EMBRACE YOUR AWESOMENESS

Feel in Control and Be Your Best Self
in this Banana-Pants Crazy World

-A *Nourish Your Soul* Book-

Julie Schooler

Copyright © 2020 Julie Schooler, BoomerMax Ltd

All rights reserved. No part of this publication may be reproduced, distributed, or transmitted in any form or by any means, including photocopying, recording, or other electronic or mechanical methods, without the prior written permission of the publisher, except in the case of brief quotations embodied in reviews and certain other non-commercial uses permitted by copyright law.

DISCLAIMER

This book is designed to give readers some useful tips and ideas. It does not replace expert advice from medical or behavioral specialists. It is recommended that you seek advice from qualified professionals if you are concerned in any way.

*This book is dedicated to Chrissy.
You effortlessly embrace your awesomeness. I feel incredibly fortunate to have been your friend for 25 years. Thanks for dragging me to that first dance class.*

CONTENTS

Reader Gift: The Happy20	ix
1. Are You Homesick For Yourself?	1
2. It's Now Or Never	5
3. The Lizard And Our Need For Certainty	15
4. The Two Primary Fears	25
5. The Four Hazards	35
6. Awesomeness Makeover	51
7. Self-Love	61
8. Security And Control	73
9. Social Awesomeness	85
10. Step Out Of Your Comfort Zone	99
11. The Paradox Of Awesomeness	111
12. A World Of Awesomeness	115
Appendix	119
Reader Gift: The Happy20	125
About the Author	127
Books by Julie Schooler	129
Acknowledgments	131
Please Leave a Review	133
References	135

READER GIFT: THE HAPPY20

Part of embracing your awesomeness is remembering to squeeze the best out every single day. To remind you of this, I created:

THE HAPPY20
20 Free Ways to Boost Happiness in 20 Seconds or Less

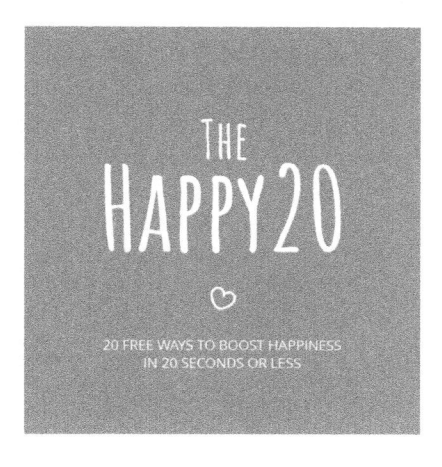

A PDF gift for you with quick ideas to improve your mood and add a little sparkle to your day.

Head to **JulieSchooler.com/gift** to grab your copy today.

AWESOMENESS ALERT!
When you enter your details for The Happy20 gift you will now get a second bonus gift.
This is an Awesomeness Pep Talk - a one-page PDF designed to be printed out so you can read it often.

Don't wait. Grab BOTH gifts today!
JulieSchooler.com/gift

1
ARE YOU HOMESICK FOR YOURSELF?

> *'To be yourself in a world that is constantly trying to make you something else is the greatest accomplishment.'* – Ralph Waldo Emerson

IT'S TIME TO REMEMBER JUST HOW AWESOME YOU **really are…**

- Know how to eat, exercise and sleep well but just don't do it?
- Are you feeling overwhelmed and out of control every single day?
- Want to be more assertive and confident but don't want to appear unkind?

This book gets to the heart of why we know what to do to have an amazing life but stop ourselves from being fulfilled and successful. It delves deep into why we are ridiculously busy, easily distracted and not reaching our true potential. And it provides answers as to why we don't go to bed on time, ask for a promotion and say 'no'.

The latest wisdom from researchers, self-help experts and prosperous, happy people cuts through the confusion around stepping out of your comfort zone, provides compelling reasons for how habits can beat procrastination and explains how to stop worrying what others think.

This is a clear, uplifting guide that will immediately help anyone who is struggling with day-to-day life in this banana-pants crazy world.

WATCH OUT FOR HAZARDS

My bestseller, *Rediscover Your Sparkle*, provides 'sparkle strategies' to fill your cup back up so you can face every day with a smile. And my book for mamas, *Crappy to Happy,* gives step-by-step guidance on how to overcome negative thought patterns, deal with emotions and reach all three tiers of happiness.

After writing those two books, I wondered what more could possibly be written on the topic of living your best life. The conscious act of getting honest with myself and admitting my life still didn't stack up to my expectations made this book take shape. I still get angry and shout. A lot. I often don't think the nicest things about my body. And I can get swept away by worry about my family, friends, finances and this banana-pants crazy world we call home.

Embrace Your Awesomeness builds and expands on these two books and is also fantastic to read on its own. It details four main types of hazardous thinking that prevented me and potentially prevent you from being our best selves: perfectionism, procrastination, people pleasing and playing small. Then it directly explains how to eliminate and minimize these hazards with an 'awesomeness makeover'. You will learn how to increase your self-worth, speak up without fear of criticism and find shortcuts to feel more in control.

I thought about not writing this book as I have certainly not mastered all this stuff myself yet. But then I would be going against exactly what this book is about: stepping out of your comfort zone, being authentic and creating new work regardless of the outcome.

Again, I have written the book I want to read.

I hope you come with me on this journey to start living a truly outstanding life.

Benefits

Follow the short, chunked down chapters in *Embrace Your Awesomeness* to:

- Stop being homesick for your deeper self
- Bust myths around willpower and motivation
- Act confidently even if you have low self-esteem
- Love yourself even though that may sound excruciating
- Use simple daily rituals to feel in control in this uncertain time
- Learn how to overcome perfectionism, procrastination and people pleasing
- Feel like you are living the life you were meant to live, one with excitement, meaning and true joy

Simple, Subtle and So Worthwhile

Writing this book and putting into practice these concepts has led to a deeper bond with my husband, an innate confidence in my ability to tackle anything from parenting to business, and a transformation in my relationship with my body.

Life is much simpler than we are led to believe. The changes seem subtle, the concepts are almost intangible, but these really are the most important things. They are what make life worth living.

Ready for profound advice wrapped in a few laughs?

If you take even a pinch of wisdom from this book, it is guaranteed that you will feel in control, thrive in a banana-pants crazy world and give yourself the best gift of all—reaching your true potential.

Embrace Your Awesomeness Today

Where could eliminating exhaustion, resentment and guilt from your life lead? Imagine being at your absolute optimum no matter what. What's stopping you from embracing your awesomeness today?

It's time to get out of your own way.

Read this book and step into the power and brilliance that you know you have deep inside.

2
IT'S NOW OR NEVER

> *'Today you are You, that is truer than true. There is no one alive who is Youer than You.'* – Dr. Seuss

THE QUARANTINE BLUES

As I write this book, the world is in the middle of the largest global pandemic we have seen in our lifetimes. This invisible plague has impacted everyone. People all over the globe have lost their jobs, their health and their lives. The virus that has swept the world has driven dramatic changes in how we work, live and interact with others.

I am one of the lucky ones. My family and I are healthy, we still have a roof over our heads and food on the table each day. But if you had told me at the start of this year that all the travel I had planned would be cancelled, I wouldn't be allowed to walk along my favorite beach, I would have to homeschool my children and couldn't hug people I loved, I would have laughed at the absurdity of it all.

But here we are.

Stuck at home with my family for weeks on end meant I couldn't fall back on my usual distractions of travel, shopping and socializing. I could be entertained by dozens of funny memes, binge-watch the next big thing or doom scroll the latest pandemic updates, but all that gets dull after a while. Yes, the kids need me and I can always enjoy a good book, but if the fundamentals aren't right and the frustrations, fears and unfulfilled feelings are still there, it is no longer acceptable for me to dismiss them.

When all that fun, superfluous and distracting stuff gets stripped away what's left is the real substance of life. The important things that truly matter. How you communicate with your partner. The relationship you have with your kids. The thoughts and feelings you cultivate on a daily basis. What your life looks like and how you want it to be.

This book is about what happens when you don't get what you think you want and instead get what you really need. This is your opportunity to consider how to make the most of, and commit to loving, your one and only life.

This won't happen overnight, but what could be more worthwhile?

And I must admit, the wisdom in these pages is not a panacea. Your life won't be perfect. But even a slight shift, even a one percent change, will help you tap back into your awesomeness once again.

It's not the most glamorous work but it is, without doubt, very rewarding.

Definitions

What do I mean by embrace your awesomeness? Let's get some brief definitions out of the way and then see if this book is for you. (Hint: it is.)

Awesome: traditionally, awesome means inspiring awe, great admiration, wonder or reverence. Nowadays, more informally, it means terrific, impressive, outstanding, remarkable or excellent. Any of these definitions, traditional or modern, sound great to me.

Awesomeness: the quality of being extremely good or amazingly impressive.

I firmly believe every single one of us is extremely good or amazingly impressive as a birthright. We don't have to be or do anything in particular to be awesome. We are already awesome because we are here on this planet. I don't want, for one instant, for you to think that embracing your awesomeness means you have to change yourself into someone else.

Embrace your awesomeness means clearing away the culturally conditioned clutter, the learned negative thought patterns and the shame of somehow not living up to some lofty idea, and simply being the best person you were born to be. It is becoming untethered from societal norms that keep you small. It is not about fixing you as you are not broken.

It is about becoming the real you.

Being awesome, in the context of this book, means accepting and loving yourself just as you are PLUS accepting that you are here to reach your potential. You can love your body and want to lose weight. You can enjoy your job and want to become the vice president of the company. You can feel content in your marriage and want to be swept off your feet on a romantic date night.

These two concepts may rub up against one another, they may seem like a paradox, but you can accept them both. Think of them as the flip sides of the same coin. Life loves presenting us with paradoxes and receiving them with grace is a helpful strategy to learn.

Ultimately, appreciating your imperfectly awesome self will allow you to grow into who you were always meant to be, reach your potential and share your gifts with the world.

I can't think of anything more meaningful to do with your life. Can you?

Who is this Book For and Not For?

Initially this book was going to be written with mamas in mind but with the global pandemic going on, it was just too important to narrow down its focus. This book is for anyone, 9 to 90, who is struggling. You are not sure what day it is, let alone how you are supposed to make the best of it.

Who is this book not for?

- Someone who is truly happy and content with their life
- Negative or pessimistic people who are not prepared to change

Read this book if—like me—you:

- Feel like you are lost in the day-to-day
- Can't just settle for a mundane life on autopilot
- Have a repetitive, persistent thought of 'Is this it?'
- Know there must be more to life than how you are living it
- Don't know who you are anymore (or perhaps never knew)
- Want to NOT feel tired, overwhelmed, stressed out and stuck
- Have a hunger inside of you, a longing for more meaning in your life
- Want to reconnect with the core you that whispers to you now and then
- Are up for a challenge and willing to experiment a little with your life to bring back your awesomeness

Please note that if you are going through a diagnosed medical issue, chronic sickness, a life upheaval or a tragedy, there are more suitable books and resources out there to support you, although the tips in here can help as well. And if you suspect your issues may be coming from a more serious cause—perhaps an undiagnosed mental or physical illness—I don't want to diminish the seriousness of your situation. Please seek appropriate professional advice.

Still here? Great! Let's get this party started.

Passwords and Ice

A couple of years ago, the expert who was tasked with prescribing the best practice for computer passwords stated that most of his advice was completely wrong. You shouldn't change your password every 90 days or use strings of meaningless letters, numbers and symbols. This just frustrates users and can be easier to hack! The current advice is to not change your password unless you believe there has been a security breach and to use a string of correctly-spelled words instead of a nonsensical jumble.

What do you do with a very sore muscle or strain? Put ice on it? Recently, a meta-analysis of scientific papers in the area of athletic injuries stated there was insufficient evidence to suggest that ice helps. The doctor who first promoted ice along with rest, compression and elevation ('RICE') even says ice may delay healing. Either rest or move the injured part of your body as you see fit, but never, ever ice it.

I was in my late thirties before I found out that there is a small arrow next to the fuel gauge in my car that tells me what side the fuel tank is on, how to properly open a Oxo cube packet, and that there is only supposed to be one space after a period, not two.

The following is attributed to Mark Twain, but, ironically, I am not sure if he actually said it: "What gets us into trouble is not what we don't know. It's what we know for sure that just ain't so."

These stories illustrate that no one really knows what they are doing, even so-called experts. Nobody has it all figured out. When you think about it, this is life. How on earth would we know what to do for our entire lives in every circumstance? We learn and grow by trying, seeing what fails and what works and doing more of the latter. All of life is built on people who are not sure but prepared to take action regardless of the outcome. This is what makes life interesting.

Our deep need for safety, certainty and predictability is discussed in the next chapter, but know for now that your quest for the 'truth' is perfectly normal AND it is not really helping you. Approaching life like a fun game or rough experiment is not easy, but it is beneficial in the long run.

If you get nothing else out of this book, then instead of asking, 'Is this true?', ask 'Is this helpful?'

I get it, you may not want to adopt these ideas just yet. They are planted here as seeds and the book will grow them out further. For now, remember this story as told by the late educator and speaker, Sir Ken Robinson, in one of his fantastic TED talks. Once upon a time, there was a music teacher in Liverpool in the mid-twentieth century who had two of the Beatles, George Harrison and Paul McCartney, in his class. He didn't think either of them had any real musical talent or potential as musicians.

Why Me?

I was extremely reluctant to write this book as I certainly don't have it all figured out, but then I thought about all these stories and realized I had to. The only question to answer is, would the book be helpful? And of course, even if the only person it helps is me, the answer is yes.

I hope some readers come along for the ride. But even if I am the only one who relearns how to navigate life's paradoxes including how to enjoy the day-to-day while also trying to reach my potential, this book is worth my time and effort.

Writing the book, in itself, is the embodiment of embracing my own awesomeness. I can't tell you to be vulnerable, step out of your comfort zone and show your creative side if I am not willing to do it. I need to walk the walk too.

Why me? Why NOT me?

While we are on a roll of quotes that may or may not have the right attribution, as Gandhi perhaps said: "Be the change you want to see in the world."

Why Now?

This pandemic is your invitation to embrace your awesomeness—find the real you and tap into your full potential. The whole world is banana-pants crazy. Nothing is 'right' anymore. What we knew as 'correct' is being thrown into chaos. It is time to question everything.

Yes, no one wants to go through this, but it's a worldwide wake up call.

The whole world has been knocked off its axis so it's the perfect time to take a good hard look at your life. Don't wait any longer. The world will never be the same again, so why should you? This is a global reset, unprecedented in our lifetimes, and what it means for YOU is that you don't have to succumb to culturally conditioned, and mostly detrimental, norms any more.

Nothing is the norm. Isn't that great?

This book will help you unlearn these socially-ingrained beliefs, take your life off autopilot, be present and remember your true nature. On a deeper level, we already know these are crucial aspects to a life well-lived. How to tap into them is not new, it is a relearning that brings ourselves back home, brings our awesomeness back.

If you are reading this book way into the future when this pandemic is consigned to the history books, I can guarantee that there will still be something banana-pants crazy going on in the world or in your personal life that means this book is helpful and relevant. Holocaust survivor and author, Viktor Frankl, wrote in *Man's Search for Meaning*, many years ago, "For the world is in a bad state, but everything will become still worse unless each of us does his best." Pandemic or not, the wisdom in these pages is evergreen.

We can't hide anymore. We need to play the hand we have been dealt. We have to learn to live with each other. And we really need to be kinder to ourselves.

It is never the right time so what are you waiting for?

Think of this book as your permission slip to shine.

MAXIMUM UNCERTAINTY

More than anything, the pandemic has brought about a lot of uncertainty. We don't know how long it will last. We are not sure what it means for the economy, the environment and the general health of the world. While I'm writing this, it's not known if a vaccine will be developed, whether it will work and how it could be rolled out to billions of people.

If there is anything we DO know, it's that none of us likes feeling out of control. At least you have one tool to help with that: asking whether something is helpful. More tools will be presented in the awesomeness makeover later. It's time now to understand why we dislike feeling unstable. The exact reasons are discussed in the next chapter.

3

THE LIZARD AND OUR NEED FOR CERTAINTY

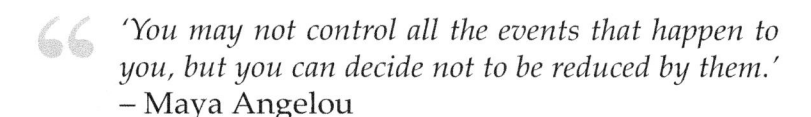

> 'You may not control all the events that happen to you, but you can decide not to be reduced by them.'
> – Maya Angelou

Prizegiving Embarrassment

In my last year of high school at the end-of-year prizegiving, I won an award for the most conscientious and diligent student. Basically, it was a consolation prize. I wasn't the top student, but I had fairly decent grades because, boy, did I work hard. I spent every spare moment studying, forsaking hobbies, family and even hanging with my friends.

At the time, I told myself I worked hard because I needed a high grade on my exams to get onto a particular university degree path. Now, I look back and see that a primary driver of studying so much was my powerful need for certainty. Studying and getting good grades gave me control over one of the only areas of my life I knew I was good at: being a great (conscientious and diligent) student.

I didn't just work hard; I worked hard to try and figure out the world. My statistics project was on winning the lottery. I was trying to find statistically significant incidences of certain numbers being pulled out. I was constantly trying to find order in complete randomness.

I couldn't control my family life—my parents had divorced a few years previously and my father was recently remarried. I didn't know what my future held—after 12 years in the school system, I was about to be thrown out into the big wide world. And it wasn't like I had been focused on much extracurricular activity—I didn't participate in sports and had no real hobbies, so I always felt like a novice, and therefore, had insecurities in those areas.

As I started to walk onto the stage to collect my prize, my mother stood up. She was sitting in middle of the full school hall with the other parents. Overcome with pride for her eldest daughter, she cry-shouted, booming over the polite applause, "That's my big girl!" Every single student, teacher and parent (it seemed at the time), turned and stared at my mother. There was a brief silence, then some laughter and finally, after what seemed like a glacial pause, a settling down with more clapping as I collected my award and scurried off the stage.

I was absolutely mortified. It was the most embarrassing moment of my teenage years. Striving for certainty over my school work led to one of the most out-of-control situations of my young life.

Now, as a mama myself, I completely understand my mother's unfiltered reaction. It is endearing just how delighted she was in her "big girl." However, it just goes to show that the universe has funny ways of throwing you into the deep end of the uncertainty pool when you are trying not to get wet at all.

THE LIZARD

We have a lizard that resides in our brains. We are evolutionarily hardwired for survival. In prehistoric times, we needed a robust flight, fight or freeze mechanism for when we spotted a saber-toothed tiger, or when it spotted us. In our heads is a little area near the brain stem called the amygdala, and it prompts us to constantly scan for anything that can kill us.

In caveperson times, anything that could kill us was usually either **scary**—large beasts with sharp teeth, or **scarce**—lack of food, water or shelter. As this is a survival tool from a primitive era, the author, coach, and wise soul, Martha Beck, describes this part of us as 'The Lizard'. Others have called it the chatterbox (Susan Jeffers), the obnoxious roommate (Arianna Huffington), or—excuse the potty mouth—the 'bee-arrcch' (me).

Let's stick with Martha Beck's description for now. The Lizard is a reptilian animal in your brain that perks its head up and alerts you to anything you perceive as scary or scarce. It does this to protect you, but it means your brain is wired to find the negative at all times. It tells you nasty stuff and is generally responsible for all your damaging thoughts, especially critical self-talk.

There are two main points here. First, you must start to think of it, whatever it is, as a separate thing. It is not 'you'. It is a tiny part of your brain pelting you with fearful thoughts and feelings. I repeat, it is not YOU. I like the idea of a lizard since I can picture it in my head.

The second main point to pick up is that The Lizard tells you things are scary or scarce even if in reality they are neither. It alters your perception. Despite the current global pandemic going on as I write this, you, in the western world, live in one of the most abundant and safe times in human history. As there is nothing really dangerous going on and you have enough to eat, The Lizard turns its attention to other things it thinks you might like to worry about.

The Lizard now tells you day in and day out that you lack time, energy, money or love. Think about that for a moment, instead of being scarce in water, food, shelter and warmth, your Lizard brain is trying to protect you by telling you that time, energy, money or love are scarce and need to be conserved. It is fake fear, but it feels very real.

You rush around like you are escaping from a predator, active and alert, but most of the rush is to escape your own worries.

You get an email from your boss saying that he wants you in a meeting in thirty minutes about that project you just handed in. What does The Lizard say to you? That you must have done a great job and he wants to give you a raise? Doubtful. The Lizard tells you that the project was not up to standard, your reputation is ruined and you are about to be fired. You get a call from school saying your eldest started a playground scuffle. What do you think first? Is he a bully? I am a terrible mother? He will now never get into college? Your partner comes home from work and turns the TV on without much of a greeting. Is he angry with you for something or is he simply exhausted? The Lizard likes to make everything personal, even if someone else's behavior has nothing to do with you. It does this to protect you, but in doing so it fills you with negative and fearful thoughts.

The good news is that you can override The Lizard, your primitive alarm system. First name it. Yes, name it. I named mine Penelope and she is a real bee-arrcch. She tells me all sorts of crappy thoughts and wakes me up at 3am to bombard me with them. SHE, Penelope Lizard, is not ME, and so I don't have to take her seriously. When Penelope wakes me up, I tell her that she is being silly. I shush her and tell her to go back to sleep. Works like a charm. But I am getting ahead of myself. This is not a solutions chapter. Let's continue.

THE NEED FOR CERTAINTY

The Lizard, more than anything, craves certainty at all times. It thinks our lives depend on it, so order and predictability are prioritized over everything else. As a survival mechanism, this has kept humanity from being wiped out for thousands of years. It is designed to protect us, and it does a great job of that.

Certainty in itself is not all bad. After all, it is a need for certainty, to try and figure things out, that has driven me to write this very book! My inner study nerd, hard at work, again. Of course, it's important to have controls around how much money you spend, have a routine bedtime and not allow your kids ice cream for breakfast every morning. Having a daily schedule, putting limits on your screen time and attempting some exercise regularly are all modern ways that certainty makes life easier. We need to believe that the cars on the other side of the road will stay there.

But this underlying need for security, although helpful to a degree, can be harmful. In this contemporary world, all that focus on certainty—safety, security, control, predictability and comfort—can come at a great cost.

There are many ways certainty can be damaging. Let's focus on three big impacts in this chapter.

Certainty versus Your Body

Just the impact on your body alone could fill a thesis. Let's check in on how you are. Right now, unclench your jaw, drop your shoulders and relax your tongue. Were these parts tense? How is this helpful?

Craving certainty drives us to blindly adhere to rules and conventions rather than listen to the inherent, but awfully quiet, wisdom of our bodies. We learn to finish everything on our plate rather than stop eating when we feel full. We let our negative thoughts and outside influences override our intuition. And we binge-watch the latest must-see late into the night rather than trudge off to bed.

Our tight need for control keeps not only our behaviors, but our bodies firmly rigid. This is obviously not good for us.

Certainty versus Variety

The universe is quite crafty, so along with certainty, we all also have a strong need for variety. This is the paradox of happiness. As discussed, the universe loves a good paradox. But novelty can take a back seat when certainty drives our lives.

In my mid-twenties, a kind but firm friend dragged me along to dance class. I hadn't taken any dance lessons in my entire life. The Lizard was telling me that I would never pick up the steps, was likely to trip up and basically look stupid the whole time. Instead, I noticed that almost everyone else was new to this type of dance and after a few stumbling lessons, I started to enjoy myself. I never got to competition level, but I can still pull out a few Ceroc moves on the dance floor when the opportunity arises. I wouldn't have this confidence if I hadn't literally taken that first step.

How often have you decided not to try that new activity, travel somewhere different or start a conversation with a stranger at a party because it seemed too scary?

CERTAINTY VERSUS HAPPINESS

When I wrote *Crappy to Happy*, the central theme was that being happier is harder than not being happy. As I explained in that book, this is due to our prehistoric survival instincts - yes, The Lizard. Humans are good at building brain structure from negative experiences but poor at doing the same with positive ones.

Now I think there is even more to it. Our need for certainty costs us a great deal of happiness. Not just because we won't try new things but because it constantly directs us back to our emotional home, the emotional state in which we feel most comfortable. You would think that everyone would prefer to have a content and happy emotional home, but that is not the case. As researcher, author and TED talk speaker, Brené Brown, states, when we lose our tolerance for discomfort, we lose our capacity for joy.

We find our way back to our less-than-stellar emotional home all the time. We complain to our friends endlessly about our partners instead of having the much-needed direct conversation that resolves the issue. We stay in a monotonous job as boredom is often a preferential emotion to ambition with a chance of failure. It helps answer why people vote for the party they 'always vote for' despite disagreeing with its current policies. Especially under times of stress, scurrying back to our emotional home makes us feel safe. How else do you explain why we worry so much?

In some twisted way, holding onto our worries makes us feel in control.

As author and therapist, Harriet Lerner discusses in *Why Won't You Apologize*, sometimes it is easier and more comforting to hold onto old resentments. You may not want to show you are doing okay as showing how hurt you still are proves just how badly you were treated. Anger can protect you from feeling where the real hurt lies including the responsibility you may have in it. Plus, it can keep alive the fantasy of justice with the wrong doing you have suffered.

Knowing that 'death and taxes', are the only two things we can rely on is strangely comforting. No wonder one of the top five regrets of the dying outlined by nurse and author, Bronnie Ware, is "I wish I had let myself be happier."

Tip the Scales

What do we do about this? It's all about tipping the scales in our favor so we get more of the right kind of control plus way more variety and happiness despite the inherent vulnerability and uncertainty that is associated with these lofty concepts. Exactly how we can do this is covered later in the awesomeness makeover chapters.

You may be annoyed at yourself, but remember that this chapter is simply about awareness. Don't judge your past self. Not only do you have The Lizard and its frenzied need for certainty to deal with, but also some built-in fears.

4

THE TWO PRIMARY FEARS

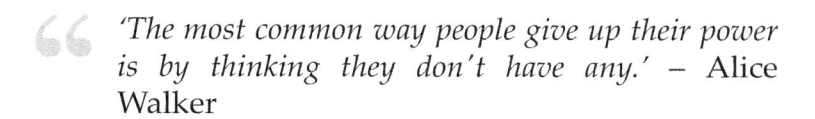

> *'The most common way people give up their power is by thinking they don't have any.'* – Alice Walker

SELF-HELP DANCE PARTY

A few years ago, I was fortunate to attend author, coach and personal development expert, Tony Robbins' signature event, Unleash the Power Within (UPW) in Sydney, Australia. If you haven't attended, it's unlike any other conference you have ever been to.

Despite the four days being long—it was the norm to return to the hotel after midnight—it was not boring for a single second. When we were not dancing to the booming music, we were frequently instructed to high five and hug fellow attendees. Every hour or two, long lines of strangers massaged each other's shoulders. There was even an opportunity to participate in a fire walk. In a nutshell, UPW was designed to make attendees feel relentless uncertainty and still feel good about it.

UPW may have a reputation as a kind of self-help dance party but it also profoundly conveyed a number of life lessons including the concept of 'The Six Human Needs'. As discussed, we have a need for **certainty**—to feel safe and secure and to know that our expectations will be met. In apparent opposition to this, we have a need for **variety**—to have surprises and spontaneity in our lives. We also have a need for **significance**—to feel important and that our lives have meaning. On the other side of the coin, we have a need for **love and connection**. The other two needs are for **growth** and **contribution**. This is an extremely concise description, and I encourage you to look up these needs in more detail. There are some great videos on YouTube on this topic. How you try and meet these needs—in positive, negative or neutral ways—plus which needs you emphasize, have a major impact on your life.

After learning about these needs and determining which ones were most predominant, a survey was done across the large crowd. If they were being honest, approximately 80% of the 5,000 attendees had the need for certainty at the top of their needs list. And of the thousands of us who had placed certainty at the top, *every single one of us* desperately wanted certainty to be not as important as the need for love and connection.

Certainty and the Two Primary Fears

Certainty helps us survive, but as we can see with the examples around it reducing variety and happiness, it doesn't allow us to thrive. No illustration of this is more apparent than in its impact on relationships. There is a reason why psychologist, Abraham Maslow, put the need for safety before the need for love in his influential hierarchy.

Think about it, have you found fault or blamed your partner, even though in showing you were 'right', the relationship was damaged? Why do you reply to just one more email to get your inbox in order when your child is waiting for you to play? It is almost a cliché to think of the executive who stays late at work (something he or she can control) to escape a tumultuous home life. It is worth noting that one of the other top five regrets of the dying was, "I wish I hadn't worked so hard."

Why is it that our connection with loved ones is jeopardized so much when certainty is involved?

What The Lizard —which is supposed to be there to protect us—constantly tells us boils down to two primary fears. We fear that:

1. we are not enough and (as a result)
2. we won't be loved.

These fears are learned in childhood and reinforced over our lifetimes by our family relationships (even the most loving ones are not perfect), school, work and society in general. In Tara Brach's book, *Radical Acceptance*, she describes the Dalai Lama not understanding what the concept of 'self-hatred' was when asked about it by a meditation teacher. Maybe if you grow up in extraordinary circumstances these fears are not formed, but almost everyone has them.

This chapter aims to get a better awareness and understanding of these two primary fears. The second half of the book will provide wisdom and tools to unravel, counter or minimize them.

The Fear of Not Enough

The fear that we are 'not enough' can be hard to grasp. Not enough for what, for whom? Susan Jeffers in her classic self-help book, *Feel the Fear and Do it Anyway*, explains that the fear of 'not enough' is the fear that 'I can't handle it'. 'It' being the situation at hand.

What stops us from living a successful and fulfilling life is the 'I am not X enough' belief. Replace 'X' with your lizard brain's favorites. Common ones are not young enough, not old enough, not thin enough, not rich enough, not pretty enough, not smart enough. Next time you stop yourself from doing something that would ultimately benefit you, pause and ask yourself gently what 'not X enough' and thus, what 'I can't handle it' belief is behind it. For example, 'I am not old enough to be the team manager' could mean that you don't feel like you have the skills, experience or maturity required to take on the new role. Half the battle is figuring out exactly what The Lizard is telling you amongst all its general, negative chatter, so try to do this with as little judgement and with as much curiosity as you can muster.

We also think there is 'not X enough' externally. Not enough time, money, energy. Nothing for dinner. Little opportunity to play with the kids. Always tired. Marketers tap into our 'not enough' fear, and use phrases such as 'bargain', 'clearance sale', 'today only' and 'just 5 left' to convey scarcity when there really is none.

Activist and speaker, Lynne Twist, has the best illustration of 'not enough'. She states that for many of us, our first waking thought of the day is 'I didn't get enough sleep' and the next one is 'I don't have enough time.' She then goes on to say that, "before we even sit up in bed, before our feet touch the floor, we're already inadequate, already behind, already losing, already lacking something. And by the time we go to bed at night, our minds are racing with a litany of what we didn't get, or didn't get done, that day."

In *Daring Greatly*, Brené Brown says that the opposite of scarcity, which The Lizard is trying to protect you from, is not abundance. It is simply 'enough'.

Your lizard brain is trying to help you but it is preventing you from accepting your true self.

The Fear of Not Being Loved

As babies we need connection and attachment to survive our first few years. We associate staying alive with needing love. An unfortunate side effect of The Lizard's job is that it creates a fear-based belief that we won't be loved. As adults we don't need love to survive (although it's preferred). However, thanks to The Lizard we think we are scarce in the one thing we have the greatest fear of losing.

Thus, we scramble to get what we think is love and connection in any form that is offered, even if it is doing more to hurt us. This goes a long way to explaining why women and men stay in violent relationships but it also helps us understand other detrimental behaviors like people pleasing and playing small (more on these in the next chapter).

In other words, we strive for love because The Lizard creates fake fear that tells us that our lives depend on getting love. Instead, we often only get comfort (certainty) as the last thing we want to do is to expose our vulnerability. These are powerful concepts and they are hard to accept, but please don't dismiss them.

Believe me, I also don't want to think of myself as an anxious person driven by The Lizard who seeks out love at any cost, but some of my behavior conveys this so perfectly there is an obvious truth to it. When, late in the evening, I stand in my dark kitchen bathed in the light of the refrigerator, I have to own up to the fact that the sweet thing I am craving is probably not contained inside it.

Jennifer Pastiloff writes in her wonderful memoir, *On Being Human*, that she thought for certain that loving someone fully would kill her, that it would cause her body to rupture. Maybe not everyone feels quite that strongly but if love is associated with losing yourself, figuratively or literally, no wonder we prefer certainty.

The Equation

The bottom line of The Lizard + Certainty + Primary Fears equation is low self-love. Remember, this whole equation is not YOU, just a culturally constructed problem that you can dismantle. Removing parts of this equation means getting back in touch with who you really are, loving yourself no matter what and living a life of freedom and joy.

It means embracing your awesomeness.

First, we need to get clear on what self-love is and distinguish it from similar concepts. Here come the definitions.

DEFINITIONS

Self-love: appreciation, regard or belief for your own worth, value, happiness and wellbeing

Self-worth: a sense of one's own value or worth as a human, or, as described by Adia Gooden in her TEDx talk, 'Cultivating Unconditional Self-Worth', "the sense that you deserve to be alive, to be loved and cared for and to take up space."

Self-esteem: confidence and belief in your worth, value and abilities, often used interchangeably with self-respect

Self-confidence: trust in one's abilities, qualities and power

When I wrote *Find Your Purpose in 15 Minutes*, I found myself in a research rabbit hole. I was trying to distinguish between purpose, meaning, destiny, mission, fate and a calling. Now, I find myself with the same issue.

Do me a favor and read those definitions again.

I don't know about you, but I can't see a whole lot of difference between self-love, self-worth, self-esteem, self-confidence or self-respect.

But what does it really matter? We tend to trip up on language and stop ourselves from seeing the bigger picture. Let's spend as short amount of time as we can here and move on to the more important stuff–changing our lives for the better.

I can't tell you how much I didn't want the answer to the equation to be self-love. I can barely say the word 'self-love'. It sounds a little sketchy to me, perhaps alluding to a more, shall we say, *intimate*, meaning. And it's sometimes associated with vanity or narcissism.

Right up until I wrote this section, I was using self-worth or self-esteem as stand-ins. But I don't want to shy away from the real issue and the real answer. If you want, when self-love is mentioned, exchange it for a more sanitized version.

I no longer want to downplay self-love.

We all need to relearn how to cultivate unconditional self-love. You need to, as Kamal Ravikant says in his book of the same name, love yourself like your life depends on it.

A Perfect Storm

Between The Lizard, your desperate need for certainty, the primary fears that you are not enough and won't be loved, and your extreme vulnerability, it is amazing that you are even able to get out of bed in the morning and function at all! You have a perfect storm of crappiness!

Please raise one hand above your head and bend it at the elbow so your hand rests on the back of your shoulder. Give yourself a pat on the back. Congratulations, not only do you get out of bed every morning, but you are trying grow and love the awesome human you were born to be. You are to be commended.

You have also gotten through this chapter, and this is a very hard chapter! Now that you know all this stuff, there is no going back. You have woken up. The first step is awareness, which you have conquered. Your brain is a tool that you want working for you, not against you. Your thoughts, emotions and hence behaviors and habits are all within your control. Isn't this a great notion? You strive for certainty and it has been within you all along.

Before we get to how you can usher yourself into awesomeness, it is important to see exactly how this lack of self-love has a harmful impact on your life.

It's time to check in with The Four Hazards: perfectionism, procrastination, people pleasing and playing small.

5

THE FOUR HAZARDS

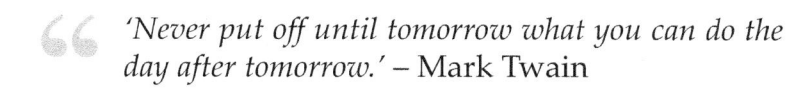

> *'Never put off until tomorrow what you can do the day after tomorrow.'* – Mark Twain

Mutant Orange Caterpillars

My friend told me this story of a time she found some monarch caterpillars in her backyard that had no food as they had eaten all the leaves of the swan plant they were on. A neighbor said he heard that feeding caterpillars pumpkin was a good substitute for the nourishment they usually get from a swan plant. This was in the days before the Internet when it was harder to check these things.

As she wanted to help out the caterpillars, my friend cut up bits of pumpkin and left it at the bottom of the stripped-bare swan plant. After a couple of weeks, she discovered that the caterpillars had morphed from their usual black, white and yellow stripes into a bright, mutant orange.

More days passed. The fat, orange caterpillars managed to create hanging chrysalises from the bare branches of the swan plant. Instead of a shiny, jade color, the cocoons looked like mini ginger blimps. Only a handful of caterpillars hatched into butterflies and the ones that did couldn't open up their wings. It was a caterpillar zombie apocalypse. My friend had the best of the intentions, but unfortunately feeding the caterpillars pumpkin, although they liked it, ultimately ended them.

Our lizard brains feed us negative thought patterns to try and keep us safe. We think these help us but they stop us from living a truly fulfilling life. We grow wonky or don't grow at all. We don't transform. And we never learn to fly.

A Diagram That Will Change Your Life

Please pay attention and study the simple diagram below as it will change your life. I am not saying these words lightly. This simple arrangement of words has the potential to have a powerful impact on the rest of your life.

Are you ready? Here goes...

> SITUATION / CIRCUMSTANCE ->
> THOUGHT / MEANING / BELIEF ->
> EMOTION / FEELING ->
> ACTION / BEHAVIOR ->
> OUTCOME

Your life is determined by the meanings you place on external events. Meanings you have decided upon. You decide the meaning. You.

The main thing to realize is that you have the power to control all the components in this diagram between situation and outcome. You often do not have the power over the situation or the outcome, but you can decide on the thoughts, emotions and actions in between. You wanted certainty, and it is right here for the taking. Because you have the control, you have the ability to also change your beliefs, choose your feelings and determine your behavior.

Once you understand that you are in control of your thoughts and beliefs, once you really get it, you will grasp just how powerful this concept is. Even believing that you have control over your thoughts is a belief in itself. Perhaps it is not 'the truth' but isn't it more empowering —i.e.: helpful—than the belief that you are simply a rag doll reacting to your environment?

In my book, *Crappy to Happy*, it was advised to pluck out a detrimental thought or belief and go about creating a different meaning around it. However, there are thousands of negative thoughts, so where do you start?

THE FOUR HAZARDS

This chapter identifies four common types of negative beliefs that keep us from living our best lives. These are The Four Hazards: perfectionism, procrastination, people pleasing and playing small. A hazard, as defined in health and safety literature, is 'a potential source of harm or adverse health effect on a person or persons.' These four hazardous beliefs have been selected as they are the most habitual yet highly destructive to our lives.

Health and safety best practice is to identify and manage the hazard. This means finding solutions that isolate and assess the hazard. Then it is about working to eliminate it or minimize it.

In this book, each hazard will be defined. Why we believe and take action on these hazardous patterns of living will be explained. There will be examples showing exactly why they hurt us. A couple of tools to help us all move past each of these hazards will be introduced.

The Four Hazards interrelate and feed off each other. Perfectionism, for example, can lead to procrastination. They are separated out here to make them easier to identify. You can then see which of the hazards you most relate to and where you want to direct your focus, at least at first.

Perfectionism

Perfectionism is striving for flawlessness accompanied by critical self-talk and worry about others' evaluations. A lot of perfectionism is wrapped up in what it is not. It is not seeking excellence, trying to attain success or wanting to master something. These reflect self-love. Instead, perfectionism is a fear-based response that if you could just control the outside world, everything would be all right internally. Jennifer Pastiloff, describing her serious eating disorder in her memoir, says that she thought if she could perfect her outside, no one would see how bad she believed herself to be on the inside.

At my first job out of university I was constantly staying late to get everything right. My manager told me that it was fine to go the extra mile but I didn't have to run a marathon. Perfectionism is trying to get to that elusive finish line because you think then you will finally be good enough.

The Lizard leads you to believe that perfectionism provides safety and protection but instead it presents you with a myriad of negative effects. Can you identify with these? I sure can!

Perfectionism:

- Keeps you busy as that 'proves' you have value
- Means being hard on yourself and overly critical when things go wrong
- Leads to never starting unless you think you can achieve 100% success
- Causes procrastination on decisions because you want them to be 'right'
- Results in difficulty saying sorry as you can't view your errors and limitations as separate from your self-worth
- Makes you think you are the only person who can do the job right so you do more than you really need and then feel exhausted
- Produces a lot of frustration, shame and anxiety even though 'perfect' people shouldn't have these emotions (perfectionists use the word 'should' a lot)

As you can see, perfectionism doesn't protect you. It does the opposite. It keeps you small, stressed and stuck. It tries to fix your lack of self-love. What happens instead, when you inevitably fall short, is a reinforcement of your unworthiness, of not being good enough.

If you want to break the perfectionist cycle of doom, you don't have to race through to the later chapters. Here a two mini-tools that will help you right now.

. . .

1. Utilize Black and White Thinking

Perfectionism is associated with black and white thinking, and this can be twisted to your advantage. Instead of striving for a perfect 10 on a range of poor to perfect, instead decide that 'perfect' means done as opposed to not done. Two choices. Not a range. Is something done? Good, check it off.

2. Chunk Down and Celebrate

Break down big challenges into bits of progress, then celebrate small wins along the way. Chunked progress toward a defined outcome is always preferential to staying late or remaining stuck.

Procrastination

I spent hours and hours collating songs for the various playlists for my wedding day. I doubt anyone even heard the 'dinner' playlist. Half the dance songs didn't get played because the speeches ran too long. I am not sure if anyone would even remember my hand-picked song that I walked down the aisle to. All that time creating wedding song playlists and not once did I do any planning for married life.

Procrastination is simple to understand, extremely common and very easy to do. In short, it is delaying, postponing or avoiding a task that needs to be done. That's all. The more interesting question is, why do we procrastinate?

The main cause of procrastination is that the completed task occurs in the future. We have to take action to attain the good feelings associated with finishing it. But the lizard brain likes comfort so we are all pleasure-seeking machines. We want to feel good now. Watching TV is more enjoyable than tidying up the house, even if you add a little guilt or stress on the side.

Unfortunately, feeling good now reinforces our feelings of not being good enough if there are more important things to do. I should know. Instead of outlining this very book —a guide that is concerned with solving the problem of procrastination—I spent over an hour watching a Beatles tribute concert!

Procrastination is insidious and can manifest in the following ways:

- Being busy
- Being distracted
- Doing the less urgent, smaller or more pleasurable tasks first
- Focusing on other 'shiny objects' rather than the important task at hand

The trouble is that all the ways that procrastinating occurs can also be justified. Perhaps you really are too busy at work to train for that marathon. Maybe you need a break and a bit of mindless scrolling helps you to relax. Often, I find that checking off a few emails and rearranging my to-do list gets me in the right head space to start writing. Occasionally, you may work out that the thing that has been sitting forever on your to-do list may not be anything you need to do. I thought I should create a podcast and when I simply removed it from my to-do list, I felt immense relief.

Try not to judge, but with a childlike curiosity ask yourself why you're not taking action on what you are supposed to be doing. Are you trying to avoid the boredom of the task? Are you attempting to numb the fear of failure? Is keeping busy a way to not do the most crucial things? These may hit home but getting honest with yourself about why procrastination keeps happening goes a long way to minimizing this hazard.

Here are two interrelated suggestions to help you boot procrastination to the curb:

1. Associate Good Feelings With Taking Action

Place more value on the emotions you get from taking action than from procrastinating. Decide that feeling accomplished is more important than short-term pleasure. Add a ton more positive feelings into the task by making it simpler to begin with or dividing it into smaller parts, then revel in milestones.

2. Associate Bad Feelings With Not Taking Action

Allow yourself to feel the guilt, stress, overwhelm and anxiety from not doing or delaying an important task. Often, we only think of the future boredom or fear, but letting in the negative emotions related to procrastinating, although not fun, is integral with living up to your expectations.

People Pleasing

People pleasing comes from our inherent need for approval, attention and affection. This is not bad in itself.

As discussed, we need these to form attachments to survive as babies. The issue with people pleasing arises when we use it to continually help us feel in control, to feel like we are enough and to feel loved.

Why do we do it? Here are three reasons:

- It feels wonderful to be appreciated (I love every single five-star book review)
- We believe it minimizes criticism and rejection (unfortunately though the one-star reviews still happen)
- And this is the big one – it means that if we are running around constantly trying to please others, we don't have to deal with our own lives (ouch!)

Wrapping your self-worth into your need for approval doesn't serve you. Here are the main negative outcomes of being a people pleaser:

- It makes you feel like you can't handle criticism or rejection
- You don't say 'no' and end up feeling resentful and exhausted
- Self-esteem bound to outside sources makes you feel less in control
- You never get what you really want as you are too afraid to speak up
- It suffocates your dreams as you try not to stand out or go for your goals
- Justifies putting relationships above your own self, like 'they' matter more
- It keeps you thinking you must be nice because you don't want to be seen as bossy, selfish, uptight or arrogant

Obviously, you need to separate your innate self-worth—knowing that you are enough and lovable just as you are—from your need for approval. It's imperative for you to be yourself. As author and therapist, Edith Eger states, "when we come to believe that there is no way to be loved and to be genuine, we are at risk of denying our true nature." Remember, you are not chocolate—not everyone has to like you.

What is interesting is that people pleasing often doesn't help the people you are trying to please. You aren't a sociopath, you do want to give to others. But there is a line where this doesn't serve you or them. If you are feeling overworked, taken advantage of and have no time for yourself, then you can bet you are not letting others take control of their own responsibilities, growth and emotions. You may even be robbing them of the vital need to help, serve or give to you.

This is true for couple relationships, in the workplace and with family and friends. And this is especially relevant for parents—of course we want our kids to be happy and have a contented life. Brené Brown says that the bravest thing we can do is let our kids struggle and experience adversity. No one said parenting was easy! This does not mean throwing them in the deep end of the pool but it does mean keeping up the swim lessons even if they don't feel like it that day.

We've established people pleasing is not good for you OR the people you want to please. Here are two ways to limit your need for approval:

1. Understand the Two Types of People

I believe there are two types of people. Those who will like you regardless and those who won't like you no matter what you do. Only listen to and hang out with the first type.

2. Say No

I've written about it in my other books but it is worth repeating here. Just say 'no'. Say 'no' nicely. Say 'no' directly. Say 'no' with humor. Say it however you can and wherever you can. Practice it. Make it a habit. 'No' really is a complete sentence. It's just so incredibly important that there will be more tips on saying 'no' later.

Playing Small

When I came back from working odd jobs and traveling overseas in my mid-twenties, I decided to retrain as an accountant. (Side note: isn't it interesting that I wanted to have a 'secure' career after so much out-of-comfort-zone activity?). I worked out I needed to study accounting for one year to get the qualification I needed. I was joining students who were in their fourth year of university. Two months after I started, all the large accounting firms initiated their recruitment for graduates for the following year. These were the best jobs available for accounting students fresh out of university. Everyone else knew this was coming but it was a complete surprise to me. I soon realized that despite knowing almost no accounting, not owning any corporate clothes and having little time to prepare for interviews, I would have to apply right away.

Striving for control at any cost and allowing fear to direct your life leads you to play small. Playing small can manifest via low self-esteem, imposter syndrome, nagging self-doubt or lack of confidence. Playing small is a good catch-all phrase for these hazards because, although they are all slightly different, there is also much overlap. And, er, I like alliteration and it goes well with the other P's. At the end of the day, they are all hazardous beliefs you adopt. They are not the 'truth' about you, they are not helpful and they are certainly not who you are deep down. Tara Brach says, "It is a waste of our precious lives to carry the belief that something is wrong with us."

Let's see what each means.

Low Self-Esteem: self-esteem is the belief you are valuable; low self-esteem is feeling bad, having a low opinion or not approving or respecting yourself.

Imposter Syndrome: an unreasonable feeling of being a fraud, that you are going to be 'found out', that your abilities have been overrated, that you don't deserve your success as it is due to luck or external factors.

Nagging Self-Doubt: a lack of faith in yourself, a constant feeling of doubt or uncertainty about oneself as a person; standing in your own way.

Lack of Self-Confidence: confidence is having enough faith in what you are able to do so that you take action; lack of self-confidence is characterized by low trust in your abilities, skills or being able to cope.

Boy do we love giving ourselves horrible labels! You may resonate with one description over another. Some terms go in and out of fashion. Imposter Syndrome is currently having its time in the sun. Overall, there is so little variation between these concepts that it really doesn't serve us to spend all day here.

Like perfectionism, procrastination and people pleasing, playing small means that we don't live up to our potential, go for our dreams or show up in the best way for those around us.

In particular, playing small means:

- Not asking for help
- Avoiding reasonable risks
- Never being happy with the work you do
- Believing you are incompetent and out of your depth
- Over preparing, which is time-consuming and exhausting
- Never feeling ready or skilled enough (see the 'enough' in there?)
- Having feelings of stress and anxiety as you are sure you will be 'found out'

You know these hazards are not serving you but the labels seem too entrenched. How do you shake them off? Here are two mini-tools:

1. PRAISE YOURSELF

Every little thing you do, give yourself a pat on the back. You want to be valued, lessen the self-doubt, not feel like an imposter? Notice all the things you do and give yourself a high five for them. It may seem ridiculous but the only way to build self-esteem back up is to approve of yourself. You are not helping the world by sitting in your own insecurities. Nourish yourself with positive feedback today.

2. Act Now

These playing small beliefs come about because you know you don't understand everything but need to act. This is a sign you are competent, not incompetent. You are enough! Imperfectly taking action is one way to forge more confidence and self-esteem. Go do that thing.

Under the guise of low self-esteem, imposter syndrome, nagging self-doubt, lack of confidence or whatever it was called, I wanted to hide away when it came to those graduate recruitment sessions. Instead, I got a friend to test me on a bunch of interview questions, borrowed a dress suit and arrived early. I ended up with four offers from four of the top accounting firms. Imperfect action wins out over playing small every time.

The Good News

This may seem like a lot to take on! Different areas of your life may highlight your people pleasing behaviors, or you may remember times when you played small. Perfectionism or procrastination or a combination of both may resonate deeply with you.

The Four Hazards are prevalent, common and detrimental but the good news is they can be eliminated or minimized. Remember, they are merely negative beliefs and bad habits. They are coping mechanisms you grab onto to help you stay above the water despite almost drowning in your need for certainty and your lizard brain fears.

They are not you.

In the second half of this book are the four solutions and their associated tools of awesomeness that will clear away these hazards. What is left after the declutter is a simple life of freedom and joy.

Ready to get started?

6
AWESOMENESS MAKEOVER

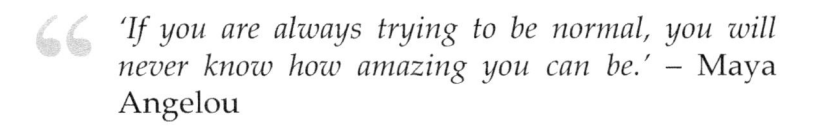

> *'If you are always trying to be normal, you will never know how amazing you can be.'* – Maya Angelou

Top of the World

Can you recall your first childhood memory? How old were you? What were you doing? I have a vague recollection of going down the slide on my first day of kindergarten when I was three years old. This stands out in my memory because that slide was wide—big enough for two kids side-by-side at once—but I didn't realize this when I started sliding down it. I tried to hold onto both sides, but I couldn't, so I held onto one side and then bumped unevenly down the short slope to the bottom. It didn't really hurt but it wasn't the whooshing glide I had envisaged it would be. I felt disappointed, a bit embarrassed and a little sore. It took the encouragement of a kind teacher to get me to play on the slide again.

At an event I went to a couple of years back we did an exercise that expanded our first childhood memory. We were instructed to go back a few moments before the actual memory began. I instantly knew what happened beforehand. I was at the top of the slide looking down, nothing in my mind except the anticipation of joy. I was on top of the world! The little girl at the bottom of the slide was the same little girl who was at the top except she had learned fear and taken on uncertainty. I know deep down I still have that little girl at the top of the world inside of me. I need to reconnect with her again.

Awesomeness Makeover

This is an 'awesomeness makeover' as it is not about changing who you really are. It's an unlearning in which you start to peel away all that negative cultural conditioning and constant lizard brain fears. Your foundation is solid, but a lick of paint and a few throw cushions would liven everything up.

This book takes what the most successful and fulfilled people do and don't do and divides them into four areas. To minimize or eliminate The Four Hazards of perfectionism, procrastination, people pleasing and playing small that are currently operating in your life, there are The Four Solutions:

- Self-Love
- Security and Control
- Social Awesomeness
- Step Out of Your Comfort Zone

Each of these four solutions will take up the next four chapters but you may have some preliminary questions. Let's tackle these.

Q&A

What if I am not sure I even want to change my life?

If you are truly content and happy, then what are you doing reading this book? If you are feeling even a little bit homesick for your deeper self, long for more nourishing relationships or constantly feel overwhelmed, then you are in the right place. Why not try the awesomeness makeover and see if it is for you? If not, you can always go back to your normal life. Remember, I am not asking you to change your life as such. Instead, this book helps you clear away the garbage so you can focus on the most important things: loving yourself and others, feeling in control and reaching your true potential.

Maybe I could do with an awesomeness makeover but can this really work? I mean, isn't everything locked up in our subconscious or something like that?

You can change your thoughts, beliefs, emotions and actions at any time. There is a fun challenge at the end of this chapter that demonstrates this. Remember the 'Is it true? or, Is it helpful?' tool? Believing that change is hard or impossible is not helpful. It is true that some of these hazardous patterns are deeply ingrained but that does not mean you can't change them. Tools such as affirmations have been shown to create new neural pathways. Tapping into your body and your intuition are direct routes to your subconscious. Taking action outside of your comfort zone builds new beliefs.

I DON'T WANT TO BE BRAINWASHED, IS THIS WHAT THIS IS?

Er, no. It takes a conscientious effort from you to change learned behaviors. This book can provide the solutions but can't do the work for you. Anyway, what have you got against brainwashing? Some brains could do with a bit of a wash!

DOES THIS TAKE WILLPOWER?

If you think it takes a ton of willpower, then you won't take action. There is a provocative notion floating around at the moment that there is no such thing as willpower. Consider that for a moment. If there is actually no such thing as willpower, then what does embracing your awesomeness really involve? I believe it involves making a decision and then building a lovable self-identity and positive habits around the new choice.

IS THIS A PANACEA FOR ALL MY PROBLEMS?

No. But if you are even one percent happier or more fulfilled isn't it worth the trouble? This is about returning to the real you. I am not saying it will be easy but it will feel right. It won't stop you from having problems but you will start to have higher-level problems.

WHAT IF I DON'T HAVE THE TIME TO DEVOTE TO THIS?

Perhaps you feel that you are far too busy, that family or work is your priority or that you are too stressed or exhausted to contemplate yet another thing you should do at the moment. And yes, like you, I lead a big, full life, but I often slide into prioritizing things that do not contribute to any real, lasting happiness. I can find myself watching a banal sitcom, shooting off an email so I can keep my inbox down and scrolling, scrolling, scrolling. Sometimes all at the same time. We all have the same 24 hours in a day, and someone out there is swimming under a waterfall, learning how to juggle or strumming their favorite song on an acoustic guitar and you are not. Are you busy being busy without adding value into your life? Our culture celebrates busyness! It normalizes stress. Don't confuse this with living a fulfilling life. Please stop lying to yourself that you are too busy—or too stressed from being so busy—to bring a bit of awesomeness back into your life.

OK, I concede that my life could be better, that this may just work and I am up for the challenge, but isn't it a little selfish?

What is selfish about wanting to become the best person you can be? What is selfish about wanting to learn and grow so can and share your unique skills, talents and gifts with the world? What is selfish about doing nice things for yourself so you can feel better and then treat others around you with respect and kindness? Do you know what I think is selfish? Allowing your need for certainty, fearful thinking and hazardous patterns such as procrastination and playing small to keep you miserable and stuck.

How can I really change unless I am hard on myself?

Author and coach, Tara Mohr writes in *Playing Big* that, "Where we think we need more self-discipline, we usually need more self-love." Working hard to get what you want is absolutely encouraged. Train for that marathon, run the race. But telling yourself you are not a success—you are not enough—unless you get to the finish line is not a healthy practice. We have to work out a way to live with the paradox that we can only be successful and happy if we are content with who we are AND also want to improve ourselves.

How do I make sure I am still thought of as a nice person?

Another way to word this is deciding that a little more confidence or self-esteem would be helpful but you don't want to be thought of as rude, bossy or arrogant. Well, you know you are a nice person, because, well, you are awesome. You can't stop caring what others think of you but can put firm boundaries up about whose opinions truly matter to you. And there are simple ways of showing assertiveness and asking for what you want without being impolite. See Chapter Nine for more.

What if this makes me stand out?

Let's get more candid and admit that what is stopping you is not the tactics or the how-to but your mindset. On the surface, it may seem strange to have fears attached to something that should be so desirable, but it's perfectly natural. After all, now you have to admit that something is missing from your life and you want it back. Any time you strive for more, for something you really want, there is fear attached. One way this shows up is a fear of attack. For instance, you don't want to stand out, be different or make a fool out of yourself in your quest to embrace your awesomeness. You want to be 'normal' but keeping to society's standards means a mediocre existence as you default to fear and negativity. Yes, this work means loving your weird self and being enthusiastic about life, even if others judge you.

What if I don't like the real me?

Now we are getting somewhere. Remember, deep down everyone is awesome. We've all made mistakes but that doesn't mean we are bad. You may not like things you have done in the past but there is still plenty of awesomeness left in the tank. Maybe the best part of all of us is the ability to grow and change. Hold onto that piece. Edith Eger writes in her holocaust memoir, *The Choice*, that our problem is "the belief that discomfort, mistakes, disappointment signal something about our worth." They don't. We deserve more than that. This is about loving the imperfect you. It is as simple as that.

What do I do about all these emotions that are coming up for me?

You can now admit you want your awesomeness back in your life. You desire it, you crave it, you need it. But here is the main roadblock: embracing your awesomeness will require you to *feel* once again. Going on this journey means getting back in touch with your positive emotions. This is hard because anyone who seems truly happy can be considered at best, naïve and at worst, certifiable. How can anyone be happy when the world is banana-pants crazy? Even more challenging: by allowing in the positive emotions, you also have to feel the so-called negative emotions—you can't feel just one type of emotion. And once you let yourself feel, you will feel everything. Everything. You will feel sad that you didn't do this sooner, angry that you missed out on the delight and wonder of life for so long and scared that once you regain your awesomeness you could lose it again. We are so used to numbing and distracting ourselves, that acute emotions —of any type—are avoided at all costs. Being in touch with your emotions puts you in a vulnerable state and this can be incredibly uncomfortable. The only thing you can do is feel your feelings. Let them pass through you and they will eventually dissipate. There is no need to be scared of them. You are enough and you can handle this.

Is it okay to ask for help?

Yes. Double yes. Now you are getting it. You must allow yourself to be vulnerable so you can become stronger. Asking for support is a courageous act. Top leaders put their hands up to ask questions. The Dalai Lama was asked something at a conference and pondered it for a full minute before saying "I don't know." This is the Dalai Lama—the spiritual guru who is expected to impart wisdom at any opportunity! Asking for help or support and saying you are not sure are brave choices as you could feel shame or judgement, internally or externally. Ultimately, they are the right, or let us say—the most helpful—choices as they remind us how to feel alive.

THAT SOUNDS LIKE A LOT OF WORK... AND FOR WHAT?

Well, maybe it's not. This is an unlearning, a stripping back to what truly gives you satisfaction and joy and nothing else. It doesn't have to take years of therapy or extraordinary willpower or changing who you essentially are. All it requires is a decision to learn to live with a bit of uncertainty while trusting you are heading in the right direction.

But I get it, I am asking you to dive into unknown waters, not knowing if you will encounter mermaids or sharks. As British comedian, Miranda Hart said on a recent Facebook Live: "We follow our hearts and sometimes our dreams come true and sometimes we get cracked open by suffering." Why would we take the risk?

Trust me when I say there is a bigger life to live. A life where you are not afraid of emotions because they make you feel alive. A life where you can fall into loving relationships and know you will be caught. A life where you achieve your goals because you are not afraid of failure. I promise that you can handle the journey, even if it gets a little bumpy, because it is beautiful and worth taking.

And if this isn't enough, do it for others. Be a role model to your children, friends or colleagues. We desperately need more great leaders in the world. Why can't it be you?

TOOLS AND CHALLENGES

Each of The Four Solutions has three Tools of Awesomeness that you can adopt into your life. They interrelate and build on each other but are separated out to make them more accessible. It's suggested to find two or three tools that resonate the most and focus on those first. Add in others as required.

There will be challenges at the end of each chapter relating to the tools introduced in it. Please, please do them. Add them into your life every day for the next 30 days. Give them a try. Only a month in your long, long life. You can do it. Reading this book is one thing but action is where the magic happens. The Tools of Awesomeness may seem off-putting at first but ultimately feel good. By giving them a go, you can decide which tools you want to keep for the long term. Please do the work!

As a starter to the main course, try this challenge. Practice twice a day for the next 30 days saying the alphabet backwards. That is all. By the end of the month, observe how much better you are at it.

Now that your questions have been answered you should be amped to jump into the first of The Four Solutions. Let's embrace a bit of self-love. But first, I must talk about bats.

7

SELF-LOVE

> 'Love is the bridge between you and everything.' – Rumi

Bat in a Cage

When I was ten or eleven, I went to the local zoo with my family. It is fairly likely we got to watch the elephants and managed the right amount of badgering to secure a double scoop of ice cream but the whole day is really a blur of hazy childhood amusement. That is, except for one vibrant memory.

A lot of the zoo experience was spent trying to spot animals in their enclosures. Towards the end of the day, we came across a tall glass enclosure that held some type of bat. I went right up to the glass and looked towards the back of the pen expecting to see a bat or three hanging upside-down near the top. I placed my hand above my eyes to shade them and pressed my nose against the cold glass while I kept looking around the whole bat house trying to spot the elusive creatures. There was a shadowy plant growing at the front that was obscuring my whole view and I kept trying to look around it.

My sister, taking delight in my growing frustration, bounded up to me and pointed out the bat straight away. With long, black wings spread out around its tiny body, somehow it was perched on the glass right in front of my face. That wasn't a plant blocking my sightline but the actual bat right there, eye-level with me, with only a thin pane of glass separating us.

I gasped and jumped back. My heart was beating so loudly you would have heard it if it weren't for my sister's pealing laughter.

Self-Love is the Answer

When the topic for this book was coming together it took me a very, very long time to come to the conclusion that self-love had to be at the core of the answer. I kept looking around it, hoping against hope it would be anything but that.

No, not self-love!

It was easy to turn a blind eye to accepting self-love as a key component but I couldn't do it forever. Glacially, I focused my vision and admitted that the very thing I had been searching for was staring me in the face all along.

If self-love is the answer, how do we manifest it? It's something that we are born with—babies demand it—that is conditioned away. It is not going to naturally spring back without a conscious effort.

Self-love is a practice.

Here are three tools to bring back self-love:

- Awesomeness Pep Talk
- Self-Love Affirmations
- Practice Self-Care

AWESOMENESS PEP TALK

You are the only you there is, the only you that there ever has been and ever will be. It is a miracle of biology, timing and whatever faith or science-backed belief you hold that you have arrived on this planet in your body at this time.

You are a beautiful, magnificent, unique, extraordinary miracle.

You don't need to do or be anything to embrace your awesomeness. It is your birthright because you are alive. You were awesome at birth and have the innate potential to become even more awesome.

In the past you have done stupid things, made mistakes, hurt people, haven't treated yourself or others kindly. You may feel guilt, shame, anger, sadness. And guess what? You are still unmistakably awesome. There is nothing wrong with you at your core being. Absolutely nothing.

There is no point compromising on who you are because you are worried what others may think. You deserve to live the most rich, full life there is for no reason at all. Showing up and being whoever you are is scary but trying to fit in by not being yourself is utterly exhausting. As Brené Brown writes, "True belonging doesn't require you to *change* who you are; it requires you to *be* who you are." Isn't it great that you don't have to prove you are enough, that you can just get on with living your life?

We are meant to be different. The things that are 'wrong' with us are the things that make us unique and special. Our diversity is humanity's greatest strength.

Embrace your quirks and be your unapologetically weird self.

Being authentic means being real. It means we stop being observers on the sidelines and start participating fully in the game of life. In *The Top Five Regrets of the Dying*, the number one regret was "I wish I had had the courage to live a life true to myself, not the life others expected of me." Practice being your authentic self every single day. Find ways to be real.

You are a vital piece of the puzzle. Don't deny the world its one chance to bask in your inherent brilliance. Be exactly who you are because why not? Make space for yourself. Find and own your place in this banana-pants crazy world.

And when you do show up and finally take off that armor, you will likely be pleasantly surprised at what strengths you have and what you are capable of. "We are not on this earth to accumulate victories or trophies but to be whittled down until what is left is who we truly are" says Arianna Huffington.

You are enough. More than that: you are a fabulously awesome big deal.

You deserve the very best simply because you are here. Playwright and activist

James Baldwin sums this up: "Our crown has already been bought and paid for. All we have to do is wear it."

Embrace your awesomeness today, and every day for the rest of your one precious life.

If you loved this **Awesomeness Pep Talk** and are thinking 'boy, I would love to have my own copy of this so I can read it often', then I have good news for you! Grab your one-page Awesomeness Pep Talk PDF (along with TheHappy20 PDF) by heading to **JulieSchooler.com/gift**.

Self-Love Affirmations

My friend and fellow author, Jennifer Hacker Pearson, The Mother Mentor, asked her Facebook group, 'The Tough Mothers Village', a question. The enquiry seemed innocuous enough but it was dropped like a bomb on the busy mamas in the group. She asked, "What if, just for today, you loved yourself as much as you love your children?"

Well, the fallout was quick, painful and explosive. Responses such as "I couldn't do it…but am going to work on it" and "I will give it a shot… but it's not easy" were typical. I read this question and felt my stomach drop. Because the truth is, well, I don't love myself anywhere near like I love my kids. And there is something very, very wrong with that.

We know self-love is missing from our lives so how do we begin to invite it back in? How do we fall in love with ourselves all over again?

How do we set about loving ourselves no matter what?

First, understanding the benefits of loving yourself can help. Remember that certainty you have been craving? Well, loving yourself gives you more stability and control plus less drama and neediness as you are not relying on others to provide love to you. Self-love is the foundation that helps prop up all the other lofty goals and values you have. You can't dream big or create with passion or provide altruistic kindness without some self-love in your heart. Harriet Lerner says, "the capacity to take responsibility, feel empathy and remorse and offer a meaningful apology rests on how much self-love and self-respect that person has available. We don't have the power to bestow these traits on anyone but ourselves."

Life just works better with self-love front and center.

Next, we must treat loving ourselves as a verb not a noun, an action we need to take. A daily practice. We can't move through life and just hope the love will come. We have to invite it back in, no RSVP required. This will feel strange and not like yourself and perhaps even a struggle, but what else could be more important? If you are sick you do everything in your power to get well—rest, take Vitamin C, keep up the fluids. We are all sick with self-loathing, or at least in a chronic state of mild dislike. We need to do anything we can to make ourselves feel better.

You may not think you can love yourself now but try to starting believing in the possibility of cultivating it. Imagine, just imagine for one second if you had the fiercely-won belief of the late author and publisher Louise Hay when she said, "there is so much love in your heart that you could heal the entire planet."

And so we get to affirmations. I know, sorry, but there is no better way to start. Yes, I am talking about repeating things over and over, writing them down in a journal or staring deeply into your eyes in the bathroom mirror. They invade the mind with a conscious choice, overriding all those negative thought patterns. They create new mental grooves that you assimilate after a bit of practice.

Why not try it? I challenge you to one minute of self-love affirmations per day for 30 days. One lousy minute out of the 1,440 minutes in each day. Put on a timer. Do it after you brush your teeth at night or anchor it to another daily habit. Try a different one each day from the list below or select one that resonates and stick with that. Some of the affirmations are lighthearted, some cut deep. The trick is to say it with feeling, with intensity, like you are going to propose marriage to your sweetheart. Don't just say it, declare it or proclaim it. If you are doing it in the mirror, look into your eyes and get as close as you can. And have a bit of fun with it. Try a different pitch or tone. Whisper or shout. Smile. Move as you see fit. Try not to eye-roll. If you notice your wrinkles or grey hair, keep repeating the self-love affirmation anyway.

AFFIRMATIONS

- I love me
- I love you
- I love myself
- I REALLY love me / you / myself
- I love me / you / myself no matter what
- I am powerful, loved, loving and I love it!
- May I love and accept myself just as I am
- I love and approve of myself exactly as I am
- Love is everywhere and I am loving and lovable

If these affirmations sound too serious, here are two quick, fun ways you can give yourself a boost with a quick dose of self-love.

> 1. When you say something negative about yourself, say the exact opposite in the most over-the-top, extravagant, quixotic compliment you can think of. Praise the proverbial out of yourself. No guilt or arrogance needs to be associated with this. Repeat it three times. For example, 'Hey you, you're an absolute fox today!', 'My goodness, I've never seen you look more stunning', 'You are a beautiful, creative, intelligent winner' or (taken from the amazing book and movie, *The Help*), 'You are kind, smart and important.'
>
> 2. Talk to yourself like you would talk to your dog (or other beloved pet or tiny child), e.g.: 'Hey, sweet girl', 'Look at that beautiful belly', 'You're so clever'. You get the picture.

Practice Self-Care

I absolutely hate bubble baths. Sitting around, never quite comfortable in water that is slowly getting both cold and dirty. I shudder at the instruction you read on every wellbeing top-ten list that advocates long baths like they are a cure-all. Don't get me started on lighting candles. Gah. Maybe it is the advice to take a bath at the first sign of stress or perhaps it's simply my reluctance to embrace self-love in all its forms, but it probably comes as no surprise that I have always cringed at the term 'self-care.'

What I didn't realize until now is that I have been encouraging self-care for a long time, throughout all my books. The entirety of *Rediscover Your Sparkle* is about self-care. I just called it 'sparkle strategies.'

The definition of self-care is simply caring for yourself. It is deliberately taking action to assist your health and wellbeing. It is giving yourself kindness, compassion and grace. There is nothing more loving than that. Self-care is self-love in action. It is as vital as the air you breathe. It provides you with feelings of more time, energy and abundance. You deserve as much self-care as you can get. Writer and activist, Audre Lorde said "caring for myself is not self-indulgence, it is self-preservation."

How to go about it?

The trouble is that self-care can take many forms. It may mean binge-watching the latest drama or switching off the screen and going to bed. It could mean going for a run or playing with the kids or snuggling up with a good book. It could mean sharing a bottle of bubbles with your friends or swearing off alcohol for a time. It could mean no sugar and it could mean indulging in that expensive box of chocolates you were given for your birthday. Self-care will look different across the days and years.

The actual form self-care takes is up to you. How do you decide? Self-care is about feeling good from the inside out, not just the Instagram-perfect outside.

In order to work out what you really need, ask yourself any of these questions. The self-care form will arise from the answers:

- What would a wise person do?
- What would my future self want me to do here?
- What would I do if I were to treat myself like the precious human I am?
- From *Love Yourself Like Your Life Depends On It* - If I loved myself would I do this thing?

Here are general categories of self-care with some specific activities that help me by making me feel in control of my body, relationships and actions. Choose what you like from the list of categories and ideas or work out your own best practices.

Category and Ideas

- Move – walk, swim, dance, yoga
- Rest – meditate, take a nap, go to bed before 10 o'clock
- Stop – take a deep breath, look at the moon, smell the roses
- Give – help out friends, practice random acts of kindness, volunteer
- Heal – talk with a trusted person and do work to mend inner wounds
- Play – have fun with the kids, play games, read a book, listen to music
- Grow – read to learn, listen to podcasts and talks, watch documentaries
- Kind – smile, laugh, be grateful, say loving things to myself and others
- Write – research, write and publish blog posts, articles and books
- Nature – go out in the sun, spend time in the garden, be in nature

- Connect – talk, listen, hug, share a meal, spend quality time with people
- Excite – waterslides, rollercoasters, trying a new activity, e.g.: disc golf
- Indulge – TV, travel, shopping, beauty treatments, go to a movie or show
- Nourish – eat lots of vegetables, drink water, and take the utmost enjoyment in a delicious and nourishing variety of food

Self-care is also wrapped around the suggestions in the following chapters. Saying no, building healthy habits and scheduling in some time to create are all forms of self-care. They are not the traditionally soft and fluffy forms like a lot of those listed above, but they are just as important.

START OVER

The most important part of giving your beautiful, magnificent, unique, extraordinary self the most love and care you can possibly handle is to not beat yourself up if you fail miserably at it! I have to admit I started mirror work when I began writing this book and then it fell away until I got to this chapter. So, I started it again.

Get up tomorrow, look in the mirror and tell yourself you love the person looking back.

Now you have embarked on bringing back the love, see how you can allow certainty into your life—the right way.

Challenges

Try these challenges for the next 30 days and then decide which ones you want to continue with for the long term.

Challenge 1 – Awesomeness pep talk: read the awesomeness pep talk to yourself once per day.

Challenge 2 – Self-love affirmations: say self-love affirmations to yourself in the mirror for one minute per day.

Challenge 3 – Practice self-care: make a list of your favorite self-care activities and commit to doing at least one per day.

Bonus 'Anytime' Challenge – Decide on your go-to extravagant compliment. Write it down and say it out loud three times whenever you are being critical of yourself.

8

SECURITY AND CONTROL

> *'There is a comfort in rituals, and rituals provide a framework for stability when you are trying to find answers.'* – Deborah Norville

THE CASE OF THE MISSING KINDERGARTEN FAREWELL

When the pandemic lockdown came in March 2020, it was swift and stringent. Kids were sent to school on a Monday like normal and by the end of the day they were told to go home and not come back for at least a month.

Unfortunately for my daughter, Eloise, the lockdown put her in a predicament, a no-mans-land between kindergarten and school. She was turning five in a few weeks which means, here in New Zealand, that she was due to finish up at kindy and go to school. In the end, she started school two weeks later than planned, not a big deal in the scheme of things. What was extremely upsetting for me (thankfully not so much for my daughter), was that Eloise didn't get to have her kindergarten farewell celebration.

I know this doesn't seem like a major concern, what with a deadly global pandemic to worry about. But of all the things that the strict quarantine caused, my daughter not being able to say goodbye properly to her kindergarten family is what kept me awake at night. A few years back, my son, Dylan, was able to make his crown, blow out the candles on his mini-birthday cake and get the 'happy birthday' and 'happy school days' songs sung at his farewell. I even have faded photos of my own kindergarten goodbye.

Luckily, after Eloise started school, we arranged for her to skip out early one Friday and go back to kindergarten to say goodbye properly. It was a wonderful celebration, complete with crown, cake and songs. To be honest, Eloise was impartial about it, fully engaged in school already, but I absolutely needed it, for the sake of a good night's sleep, if nothing else.

Finding Positive Ways to Be in Control

Finding ways to feel in control of your life is vitally important. As we have seen, striving for too much certainty has its downsides, but taking the reins helps you feel safe. In fact, feeling in control of your life is proven to be linked with more success, health and happiness.

We just need to figure out how to do it the right way.

The first thing that helps is understanding that there are tons of things that we have complete control over.

Here is a small selection:

- Mindset – your thoughts, beliefs, emotions, attitude, opinions, perspective
- Values – how honest you are, how much gratitude you express
- Activities – the books you read, sports you play, hobbies you take up
- Social – choice of friends, asking for help, how kind you want to be
- Food – what food you put in your mouth, how often and when you eat
- Decisions – level of risk you take on, whether to try something new or retry
- Language – what you say, how you say it, when to just shut up and listen
- Body – how often you smile, move, stretch, dance or sing
- Money – how much you earn, spend and save
- Work – what work you do, how much effort you put in
- Sleep – the time you go to bed, when you turn out the lights

I get it. Some of these things may sound confronting and not at all in your control. Maybe you don't feel like you can change jobs, save the money you want or have time for exercise or sleep. Just because right now these may seem impossible doesn't mean you don't have control over them.

Life is full of stages with varying degrees of control in different areas. Parents of a newborn may not be able to choose when they sleep—believe me, I know! But one day your child will sleep through the night—hallelujah—and you will too again.

Please just start to entertain the notion that you have much more influence and power over your life than the constant barrage of news, social media and others' opinions will have you believe.

If author and holocaust survivor Victor Frankl believes it, you can too. His most enduring insight is that forces beyond your control can take away everything except for your freedom to choose how you will respond to a situation.

You can control what you think, feel and do about what happens to you.

Empowerment occurs with choice. You will always have problems, so aim for better problems! You can choose to believe something and also change your mind. When something happens, knowing you have control over whether to accept it, leave it or change it helps a lot. Remember, it doesn't matter if it is 'true', only that it is helpful.

What kept me from having a peaceful slumber when we were unsure if the kindergarten farewell event would happen was that the lockdown left an 'open loop'. Open loops occur mundanely on a daily basis and are such a seamless part of the fabric of life you barely notice them. You text someone, you put on a load of washing, you wait for the train. But if the loops aren't closed, anxiety creeps in. He never texts back, the washing machine breaks down, the train is late. One constructive way to feel in control, and reduce stress, is to close as many open loops as you can.

Here are three other, positive ways to create security and control:

- Rituals and Habits
- Empowering Language
- Tap into Your Intuition

RITUALS AND HABITS

Habits, systems, routines, traditions, customs or rituals create certainty in both positive and negative ways. You can take up smoking or take up running and you can be certain of one thing—each will have a different outcome. I prefer the term 'ritual' as it has an enlightened ring to it, but the words will be used interchangeably in this section.

Last night, five-year-old Eloise started crying and pointing at the piece of broccoli on her dinner plate. While wiping away tears, we ascertained that she was annoyed that everyone at the table got MORE broccoli than her. She wanted her fair share. Yes, she wanted extra broccoli! When I wrote about making eating vegetables a habit in *Easy Peasy Healthy Eating*, I installed it as a fixture in my own home. Every night just before dinner the kids are offered a bowl of raw vegetables. On their actual dinner plates, they often have some salad or cooked greens. Sometimes they eat them all up and ask for more. Other evenings I am told emphatically that they no longer eat carrots. In the long run, they eat a lot more vegetables, and enjoy them too, than if I hadn't started this practice.

Habits have so many benefits in addition to giving us a sense of control and predictability. People erroneously think habits deny freedom but they actually provide more freedom as they give us space to make other decisions and think creatively. They also convey a sense of mastery as doing a habit over time will improve how well you perform. If you install the routine in your life, if it is something you just do, the ingrained habit minimizes perfectionism and procrastination. Last, habits eliminate the need for willpower and discipline. If it is part of your lifestyle, then you don't need to push yourself to do it. It just happens.

Selecting and increasing the number of positive habits not only helps you feel in control but changes your life for the better. Identifying and reducing bad habits is equally important. How do you go about this? You build a habit in four steps: a cue to notice and initiate behavior, a craving to change your state and get what you want, your response which is the habit you perform, and the reward or the goal that satisfies your craving. If you want to floss every night, for example, the cue is brushing your teeth, the craving is a clean mouth feel, the response is the actual flossing and the reward is a gold star from your dentist. You are more likely to do this if the floss is next to the toothpaste and you have built it into your nightly routine. I urge you to read James Clear's wonderful book, *Atomic Habits* for a full breakdown and many examples. Don't have time for reading? Make it a habit, say 15 minutes before lights out each night.

What you want to do is identify habits that provide more certainty, that give you a feeling you are in control of your life and then make them as simple as possible. As James Clear states, "redesign your life so the actions that matter most are also the actions that are easiest to do." The self-love affirmation and self-care practices introduced in the last chapter are exactly the kind of rituals you want to make easy.

Here are two more examples:

Rituals and Traditions: Rituals and traditions feel both personal and profound. We try to eat dinner as a family most nights and when we do, we pause for a few seconds to say thank you. This is a general thank you to the food producers, the stores, whoever cooked that night and the fact we get to sit at the dinner table and have a meal together. Work out some rituals and traditions that are meaningful and install them into your life. When the world is banana-pants crazy, rituals and traditions help you feel settled.

Practical Systems: Although not so magical, dealing with practical areas of your life makes everything easier. Practices can be yearly, monthly, weekly, daily or more often. Schedule in the calendar once per year to review your life paperwork—your will, insurances and family budget. Decide on weekly meal plans. Block out a daily movement time. Make your bed each morning. Look at your own life and see where you can automate decisions and reduce friction so life doesn't feel so out of control. None of this has to be hard. Do you know how I make sure I don't lose this manuscript draft? No back up, no app, no cloud. I press save, close the document and send it to myself in an email.

Empowering Language

You are in control of whether you speak at all plus every single word that comes out of your mouth. You wanted control. Isn't it amazing how much certainty we can gain in the area of language?

Unfortunately, many of us have habitually ingrained a number of disempowering words and phrases. We use a lot of negative sounding words: 'must', 'have to', 'need to' and that perennial favorite 'should' that imply that we don't have options in our lives. This is a language of disempowerment, of busy, stressed, exhausted people who have forgotten that they have choices. We need to first be aware of this and then stop it. These are just stories we tell ourselves; they are not necessarily true and they are definitely not helpful.

Consciously reworking what you say into empowering language increases how much you feel in control of your life. Find replacement words and say them instead.

Here are some positive switches to start you off:

- I have to -> I get to
- I must -> I prefer to
- I need to -> I choose to
- Can't -> Won't
- Hope -> Know
- Never -> Lately
- Should -> Could
- Always -> Sometimes
- Problem -> Opportunity
- Just, actually, kind of -> I would like

Yes, it seems like you must take the kids to school, have to make their lunches and should get to school on time, but just play with it a bit. Try on the empowering language, say it out loud, see how it feels. You prefer to take the kids to school, get to make their lunches and could get to school on time. It may feel a bit strange but is it any less true?

How to start? Building on the habits section above, make it easy by changing one phrase at a time, perhaps the worst one in your vocabulary. Maybe 'should' and its implication that you are wrong is the one that needs to go. Also, associate positive feelings with using this new form of language. You don't have to sound stern or like a robot. Use these new empowering phrases with all the warmth and good humor you can muster.

TAP INTO YOUR INTUITION

I had some books to return so I hopped in the car to make a quick trip to the local library. Just before I backed out of the garage, without any conscious thought, I got out of the car and walked around to the rear of it. Eloise, who was about two at the time, and a few seconds before had been playing out in the backyard, was standing directly behind the car. I simply wouldn't have seen her if I had backed out as I usually did. What could have happened is too horrific for me to contemplate. Sure, maybe I saw her walk by out of the corner of my eye, or perhaps heard a noise I didn't entirely register. But I would like to believe that it was my intuition that directed me to check behind my car that day.

Intuition may seem like an odd choice to help you feel more in control, but please hear me out. First, before I explain why tapping into your intuition helps increase certainty, I want to say that it is only one tool in the toolbox. Use it in addition to other tools such as practical actions and routines. After the car incident, we put a double lock on the internal garage door and made sure we shut it every time we went out.

Intuition is poorly understood and surrounded by myths and half-truths. It's simply a knowing beyond words—the ability to understand something without conscious reasoning. Whether you believe it or not, everyone has an intuitive side. Some are more in touch with it than others. Yours is in there somewhere! It can be difficult to decipher lizard brain chatter from intuition so know that your gut won't speak to you in actual words. Instead it calmly whispers to you via your physical sensations, in dreams, having unexpected energy or pain or in strange synchronicities. It moves you in the right direction but doesn't tell you your destination, which is why it doesn't link up with that 'closed loop' feeling that you traditionally need to feel secure. When I got out of my car, I was compelled to walk behind it, even though I didn't know why. I didn't feel anxious. It was actually one of the calmest feelings I ever had until I saw Eloise standing there.

Getting back to listening to your intuition is not something to learn, but to unlearn—you must make space for it. First, practice leaning away from the need to logically make decisions and rationalize. Allow the possibility that your intuition is as good as, if not better than your frontal lobe. Second, get back in touch with your body. It's called a 'gut reaction' for a reason. Anything that strengthens the core helps with your intuition. Straighten up your posture and take some deep belly breaths throughout the day. Do this now—sit or stand up straight and take four deep breaths, expanding your stomach on the inhale and blowing out on the exhale. Last, add in a daily stillness habit: pause to breathe deeply, walk in nature, meditate or simply sit in silence and notice your five physical senses. These all help to give your lizard brain a rest and let your intuition speak.

Along with more control, a willingness to trust your intuition is associated with overcoming self-doubt, greater ease and flow and more happiness and success. There is so much more that could be said on intuition, its benefits and how to tap into it, but this section is a taster to help you pivot your understanding and to allow it some room in your busy life.

Your intuition is always, always, always, working for you.

You want certainty and it is inside of you, at the core of you, at all times. What could make you feel more secure than that?

The next chapter helps enhance the only area of your life proven to be directly linked to your happiness—your relationships.

CHALLENGES

Try these challenges for the next 30 days and then decide which ones you want to continue with for the long term.

Challenge 1 – Rituals and habits: decide to do one positive habit every day for the next month, e.g.: go for a 20-minute walk, have a bowl of raw vegetables before dinner, say thanks at every mealtime, make your bed or spend some time reading.

Challenge 2 – Empowering language: change at least one disempowering word or phrase to an empowering one, e.g.: remove 'should' from your vocabulary. Simply don't say those negative words. The Lizard might still think them, but don't say them out loud. I doubt anyone will notice as they are too busy rushing around being stressed. But you will feel a difference.

Challenge 3 – Tap into your intuition: add in a daily stillness habit: pause, breathe deeply, walk in nature, meditate or sit in silence and notice your five physical senses in order to make space for you to tap into your intuition.

Bonus 'Anytime' Challenge – Adopt some practical habits you want to set up and continue with on, say, a monthly basis, e.g.: reviewing your expenses, installing a regular date night or volunteering.

9

SOCIAL AWESOMENESS

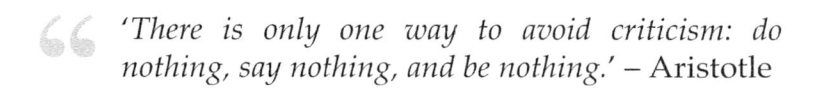

> *'There is only one way to avoid criticism: do nothing, say nothing, and be nothing.'* – Aristotle

Oprah Says No

I attended a live show with Oprah Winfrey a few years ago. She talked for almost three hours, imparting many life lessons and vibrant wisdom. One time, Stevie Wonder asked her to help out on a project he was coordinating. She was very busy with other priorities but didn't want to let her friend down or be thought of as a bad person (who identifies with this?). After days of hand-wringing, she called Stevie Wonder back and said that she couldn't assist him at this time. She expected the worst. What was the response? A simple 'no problem' from the singer. Oprah explained to the 10,000-strong audience that that was the day she learned that 'no' is a complete sentence.

. . .

BOUNDARIES

No one has yet proven that money, career choice or—unbelievably—even health, have much of an effect on how happy you are. But consistently, across many different studies, personal connections and strong social bonds have been shown to make a meaningful contribution to happiness.

Why then do our primary relationships often steer us to anger, sadness, stress and chaos? Our lizard brains, the fear that we are not enough and an excruciating need to feel loved at any cost lead to behaviors that drive away real connection. Without true bonds, our relationships function on a surface level, but the joy we seek is smothered by our poor attempts to feel safe and secure.

Paradoxically, the way to allow ourselves to be more empathetic and vulnerable in our relationships is to install strong boundaries. Brené Brown says, "Compassionate people ask for what they need. They say no when they need to, and when they say 'yes', they mean it. They're compassionate because their boundaries keep them out of resentment."

Boundaries don't constrain us, they free us.

Boundaries are simply the line where we separate ourselves from others. You can install new boundaries, uphold existing ones and move them when they no longer suit you. They can arise in many different areas including around time, money, work, thoughts, emotions and physical space. For instance, if you allow people to directly influence your feelings or you take action that prevents others from being in touch with emotions, your boundaries need to be reviewed. You are not responsible for anyone else's happiness, sadness or any other feeling. This is such a simple concept to understand but so hard to put into practice. Especially as a mama, I want my kids to feel content. However, if we take this to its logical conclusion, my eight-year-old, Dylan, would feel most happy eating ice cream and playing Minecraft all day long.

Boundaries done right allow people to grow into their best selves.

If they are so important, why don't we uphold them? Like Oprah experienced, we are worried about what the other person will think, want to avoid potential conflict and want to be thought of as a nice person. These are fears directed by our lizard brains and are perfectly normal, but they can be overcome. It's your choice: discomfort or resentment?

This chapter provides three boundary-related tools to increase connection. Done correctly, boundaries make you feel safe and in control of your life. They are another form of self-care in action. In addition, these tools help you to maintain great social interactions that keep your budding self-love, self-respect and self-worth intact.

Here are three boundary tools:

- Say 'No'
- Detach from Approval and Criticism
- Better Communication

Say 'No'

Building and upholding boundaries is such a large topic that it is easy to feel overwhelmed. Where do you start? You start by saying 'no'.

Saying 'no' after a lifetime of 'yes' will be difficult, at least at first. It takes practice and commitment. But if you do not learn to say 'no', then you are saying 'yes' to someone else's agenda and 'no' to yourself.

If you are unsure whether to say 'no' to a future commitment, ask yourself if you would do that very thing tomorrow. Tomorrow is probably already booked up solid, so if you still want to do that thing, then say 'yes', otherwise say 'no'. Remember that you never, ever want to offer a begrudging 'yes' when your gut is saying 'no'. Author and entrepreneur, Derek Sivers, says, "If you're not saying HELL YEAH! about something, say NO."

Even in the nicest way possible, saying 'no' is uncomfortable, so practice on small things and build up. Here are a few ways to say 'no' politely:

- "I apologize but that doesn't work for me."
- "Sorry but my current commitments mean I cannot take that on."
- "I can't help you at the moment but I can schedule it after X date."
- "Sounds wonderful, but that is not part of my work focus right now."
- "It sounds amazing but I wouldn't be able to give that the attention it deserves."
- "Sorry it is not my policy to do X." (People respect policies, even ones you have made up yourself!)

Another tip is to say, "Let me check my diary and I will come back to you." This gives you a buffer, a soft no. Make sure you do respond promptly, whether in the affirmative or negative. Suggesting someone else to assist also helps soften the no blow: "Connor in accounts would be the best help for that." Occasionally, offering your no with humor works. When my children ask me something ridiculous like if they can drive the car, a simple "Nope!" is sufficient.

If a no is done well, people should be happy with how clear and committed you are to what is important to you. And if they are not happy? Well, their response is their problem. Unfortunately, unlike with Oprah, sometimes the other party will respond in an attacking or negative way to your no. This doesn't happen as much as you think it might, but the possibility is there. Hold your ground! What you are doing is moving a boundary line and it is normal for the other person to not like this. After all, things then seem out of their control. But if it is important to you, gently but firmly reiterate your no response. Brené Brown says that she has not regretted increasing boundaries or a single no. The other party will soon accept the new normal or move on to someone more amenable. More on assertive communication and uncoupling from what others think in the next sections.

DETACH FROM APPROVAL AND CRITICISM

Wanting approval, appreciation, recognition, praise and compliments and avoiding criticism, rejection and conflict are deeply ingrained needs. Dale Carnegie summed it up best in the self-help classic, *How to Win Friends and Influence People*: "As much as we thirst for approval, we dread condemnation." We think we are not enough so look externally for validation. We may be met with brickbats or bouquets, but in either case we are giving away our power and control to something outside of ourselves.

I really dislike the advice to grow a thicker skin. The whole visual of a crusty casing, a hard-shell outer layer is kind of repulsive to me. How do we navigate social relationships that have the potential to wound without growing an exoskeleton?

First, we cultivate self-love using all the tools described above. We practice loving affirmations. We value being authentic. We take up self-care in all its forms. Next, we develop habits and other positive ways to feel in control. We initiate and hold boundaries. And then we can choose to take a step out of our comfort zones and let approval go in favor of being real.

Next time you want approval or are trying to avoid criticism, use these reminders to quickly get out of your own way:

- Focus on results, not approval
- Say a simple 'thanks' whatever the opinion
- Know that somebody out there needs your message or your gifts
- Don't judge or limit yourself when you don't know what others are thinking
- Consider that no one recalls what was said yesterday, chiefly on the socials
- Understand that what others think of you has nothing to do with you and everything to do with them

Building on boundaries, the most effective way to detach from others' opinions is to decide on exactly what topics, situations and people you care about.

Straight away, this eliminates all strangers on and offline, especially anonymous commenters on the socials. It also omits any topic you don't care about. If like me, you are not interested in college sports or fixing up old motorbikes, simply don't engage. Any situation in which the person with the opinion has little to no knowledge on a topic can be disregarded. I don't need a friend in financial trouble giving me stock trading tips. This may not help with specific approval and rejection per se, but it does start to build up your boundaries around who you let into your inner sanctum.

This does leave you open to the opinion of someone who you respect or who is very close to you. In the past, I was stung so hard by rejection, I didn't know which way was up. It is especially hard to take criticism if it matches some negative belief about yourself—you are not thin / smart / rich enough, that kind of thing. Strengthening your self-love muscle is always a first step.

A profound way to manage in these situations is to pivot —make it very easy to feel approval and extremely hard to feel criticism. Approval occurs almost 24/7 in my life. Whenever I express gratitude, smile or take a deep breath I feel approval. I am in charge of my own appreciation because, well, I love me and I'm awesome. I like praise and recognition from others but as the cherry on top of my ice-cream sundae. As I said earlier, I absolutely adore every five-star book review, but I would still write these books regardless.

Now, rejection happens ONLY if I were to consistently believe the false illusion that the world is mean, that everything has to be in order and that others have the power to reject me instead of knowing deep in my soul that the world has an endless abundance of love, energy and joy, that the only thing I have to do is breathe and I am the only one who determines how I feel in any moment.

I take on personal, specific, well-thought-out feedback and discard the rest. Why would I waste my precious time otherwise?

A meaningful way to drop the need for others to think well of you is to commit to a cause or venture that is much bigger than yourself. When Dylan started at a daycare close to my workplace in the city, I noticed that there was a walkway immediately adjacent to the outside play space that workers from nearby offices used as a smoking area during their breaks. Not wanting my beautiful baby boy (and all the other kids) to play in second-hand smoke, I immediately called the daycare supervisor, the building manager and the local council to see what could be done to erect 'No Smoking' signs in the walkway as soon as possible. I am sure a number of people I interacted with thought I was being dramatic / bossy / an overprotective mama, but all that mattered to me was that the cigarette smoking directly outside the daycare stopped immediately. Within a week, 'No Smoking' signs were up and my baby was playing in clean(er) air.

You get to decide if being creative, inspiring, completing a challenge or contributing on a greater scale is more important than being liked.

You have installed some much-needed boundaries via the practice of saying 'no' and restricting the situations where approval or criticism can bite you. No focus on social relationships would be complete without a look at communication.

Better Communication

Communication is a gateway to building connections, developing deeper relationships and feeling secure in them… if you get it right.

Did those suggestions of how to say 'no' politely give you a slightly sick feeling? Reread them again. Practice saying them out loud. Despite what you are led to believe, the statements are not aggressive, bossy or rude. Assuming your tone and volume is reasonable, they can only be described as warm, direct and assertive. Your objective is to up your level of warm, direct and assertive communication and reduce other forms. This is a win-win as it suggests care for both parties: me AND you. This helps you feel in control and presents your most compassionate self to the world.

There are four main types of spoken communication, best explained using examples. What is the response when a colleague asks you for your assistance on his task when you have a full load to finish today and would like to leave work on time?

- Passive: "Ok, no problem." (While seething inside).
- Passive-Aggressive: "Ok, no problem. I'll just stay late as usual."
- Aggressive: "What? No way. And don't ask me again."
- Assertive 1: "No." (It really is a complete sentence!)

- Assertive 2: "Sorry, no. I am leaving on time today. I may have a spare half-hour to help you tomorrow after lunch."

Hopefully it is obvious that assertive communication is the goal. Here are some other examples of warm, direct, assertive communication in close relationships:

- I statements: "I feel like…" rather than "You made me feel…"
- Consequences: "Please make your bed or you are not playing Minecraft"
- Ask for what you want: "Please buy milk on the way home…" rather than "We are out of milk again, why do I have to sort this out every time?"

Keeping warm, direct and assertive in your mind bodes well in all communication but especially when you have to have a tough conversation. Embracing your awesomeness means standing your ground while being as empathetic as you can. Even if resentment or frustration may seem easier, tough conversations can no longer be avoided. They are likely to be painful. But the alternative is numbing, evading and not living life to the fullest, and I, for one, am not prepared to continue along that path any longer.

It is worth noting that one of the top five regrets of the dying was 'I wish I'd had the courage to express my feelings.' Assertive communication is a great way to do this. Harriet Lerner writes in *The Dance of Anger*, using the phrase, "I am not criticizing you, just telling you how I feel and what I want" is not easy to say but a very good place to start. This may make the other person feel more out of control and emotional. Let them feel their feelings.

Don't deny them the experience of moving through their own pain. Yes, tough stuff, but growth is always better than stagnation.

Becoming more assertive does not mean becoming more argumentative. Upholding or moving boundaries often leads to what is termed 'change-back attacks'. Arguments for the most part end up with both sides being more certain of their own points of view. Essentially, our need for certainty trumps our need for love. If you strive to convince the other that they are wrong how does that help build a better relationship?

Why choose to be right instead of happy when there is no way to be right?

Instead, thank the person for bringing the point to your attention, muster all the calmness you can, listen to them fully and try not to jump in to defend yourself. Tell the other party that you want to think over their point and if you can, show them some appreciation for having a strong interest. You may not feel like doing this, but if the relationship is important to you, then it is the more loving thing to do. As Dale Carnegie says, most people want sympathy so challenge yourself to offer friendliness irrespective of what is said. Using the phrase "tell me more" when it is the very last thing you want to hear is a courageous act.

WIN-WIN

Better communication means warmly, directly and assertively speaking up for what you want and what is important to you. It is self-love in action. And it means avoiding unimportant arguments, being friendly and saying less for the sake of your relationships—love for others in the real world. Navigating these life paradoxes is not easy but there is no other way to play a win-win game in the social arena.

Empathy and compassion require you to understand and agree with other's pain. They do not require you to take it on, to load yourself up with it, to wear it as a t-shirt. The only way you can increase your understanding, empathy and compassion, which is what this banana-pants crazy world needs desperately, is to combine self-love and acceptance with strong boundaries.

Understand or try to comprehend what they are feeling but don't feel it for them. You have the right to everything you think and feel AND so does everyone else. I am the first to admit that it can be easier to sit in resentment and judgement but it is far more fulfilling to try and believe that everyone is doing the best they can with what they have and love them no matter what. At the end of the day it's all love.

Love is ALWAYS the answer even when we don't want it to be.

Throughout this book, I have mentioned the top five regrets of the dying from book of the same name. They reflect what happens at the end of our lives when we let our lizard brain fear and need for certainty take over. So far, we have:

- I wish I hadn't worked so hard
- I wish I had let myself be happier
- I wish I'd had the courage to express my feelings
- I wish I had had the courage to live a life true to myself, not the life others expected of me

The final one is 'I wish I had stayed in touch with my friends'.

What could possibly be more important than nurturing relationships in the most win-win way possible?

Let's move onto the fourth and last solution. It is the final one for a reason as it asks you to face uncertainty head on.

Challenges

Try these challenges for the next 30 days and then decide which ones you want to continue with for the long term.

Challenge 1 – Say 'no': say a polite 'no' every day—to your partner, kids, friends, work colleagues, charities, committees, sales people and anyone else who comes along. Remember 'no' is a complete sentence.

Challenge 2 – Detach from approval and criticism: practice ignoring opinions of those who do not matter (95% of the world) and saying a simple 'thanks' to any other feedback you receive in the next month.

Challenge 3 – Better communication: be vigilant at reworking as much of your communication as possible into warm, direct and assertive sentences, using I statements, consequences and asking for exactly what you want.

Bonus 'Anytime' Challenge – Use the phrase 'tell me more' when it is the very last thing you want to do during a tough conversation or argument.

10

STEP OUT OF YOUR COMFORT ZONE

> *"And you ask 'What if I fall?'*
> *Oh but my darling,*
> *what if you fly?"* – Erin Hanson

BOATY MCBOATFACE

In 2016, a British government agency asked the public to suggest a name for a new polar research ship. Appropriate names such as Endeavor and Falcon for the grand and expensive vessel were put aside when an out-of-the-box proposition became the clear front-runner. All the good people of the Internet wanted the ship, which was commissioned to carry out serious scientific exploration, to be called Boaty McBoatface.

In the end, the ship was named the R.S.S Sir David Attenborough after the natural historian. The powers-that-be did concede to the general public's whim and gave the name Boaty McBoatface to a small autonomous submarine in their fleet.

You may think this story is a red, flashing, neon warning sign against letting chaos rein. But it is the complete opposite. It illustrates just how creative, light-hearted and community-spirited humans can be when they are invited to imagine, dream and step out of their comfort zones. Isn't that what we want more of in the world?

Forecast: Uncertainty

The last few chapters have demonstrated that there is a great deal that you are in control of and that you can establish practices and habits to increase certainty over your life even further. Ultimately, though, there is and always will be an awful lot that is never going to be within your control. As the Serenity Prayer so eloquently puts it: 'Grant me the serenity to accept the things I cannot change, the courage to change the things I can, and the wisdom to know the difference.' You can check the weather forecast and take an umbrella with you but you can't stop the rain.

People don't want to leave their comfort zone as it feels pleasant and familiar, and they feel safe and in control of their environments. Going to work, coming home, watching TV, these are all nice at times. Being in your comfort zone is comfortable, but after a while it starts to hurt you. You start to feel unenthused and jaded with your routine existence.

Right now, with the pandemic going on, you may really feel like your comfort zone is the one thing you can hold onto, that you need it to survive, to just get through each day. I get it. Please don't embark on the solutions and tools in this chapter if you are barely holding your head above the water. Keep going with the self-love practices, establishing habits that make you feel more in control and deepen relationships with those close to you. When you are ready, come back here.

However, in order to live with insecurity without hiding away under a rock, you need to find ways to feel okay even when you are not in control. You need to step out of your comfort zone. This takes courage and you can't have courage and comfort at the same time. Trying new things leads to growth, and growth is necessary for a fulfilling life. Studies have shown over and over again that successful people make a habit of being uncomfortable.

You have already started to do this by attempting challenges such as self-love affirmations, tapping into your intuition and practicing saying 'no'. You have started to embrace the notion that determining if something is helpful is better than fighting for the 'truth'. You really do have agency over your decisions and can change things.

Just outside of your comfort zone is where the magic is.

Susan Jeffers sums this up elegantly in *Embracing Uncertainty*: "I relax my consciousness. I un-set my heart. I wear the world as a loose garment. I learn to dance with grace on the constantly shifting carpet."

Here are three tools to step out of—and ultimately expand—your comfort zone:

- Fail
- Create
- Dream Big

Fail

In *Super Sexy Goal Setting*, I stated my goals for the year in a book I wrote about how to write and achieve your goals, and I didn't accomplish them. I didn't just fail, but failed publicly! This is the most mortifying kind of failure.

In an attempt to recover from my failure-induced despondency I did a little digging. My research found me in good company. Many successful people have encountered failure. I can now see failure can be a rich, meaningful and, dare I say, agreeable, experience. I encourage you to fail for three reasons:

1. Failure Is a Chance to Learn What Doesn't Work

When billionaire business owner, Sara Blakely, was a child, her father would ask her over dinner what she had failed at that week. If she didn't have something to report, he was disappointed. To him, if his children weren't failing, they weren't trying.

Perhaps only half a book is written by the deadline, or the side business only makes a few dollars or the finish line is crossed well after everyone else has gone home. So what? It still means that you did better than everyone who never tried. You can do it again and do it better. You learned a lot, gained skills, and now you know what to focus on to improve next time. If you shoot for the stars and only land on the moon, you can still be proud of what you achieved.

2. Failing Is The Only Way to Get Over the Fear

Understandably, stepping out of your comfort zone is associated with a fear of failure. One way to get over that is to expect it. You will fail. Sometimes you will fall down so spectacularly hard that you are not sure if your tailbone will ever feel right again. But you will also learn to get back up, dust yourself off and keep going.

Once you fail and survive, the fear loses its grip a bit. You learn, as Sara Blakely says, "failure is not the outcome". The fear will make you think that failure means the end but it is only the beginning. Maybe next time you will fail better.

3. The Most Successful People Have Failed

All the most successful people have failed. Failed big time. This list may help you feel better about your failures:

- Oprah Winfrey was fired from her first TV job at a local news station as she was 'unfit for television'.
- J.K. Rowling's *Harry Potter* manuscript was rejected by all 12 major publishers.
- Elvis Presley failed an audition to become part of a vocalist quartet as he was told he 'couldn't sing'.
- Walt Disney was fired from his newspaper job because he 'lacked imagination and had no good ideas'.
- Michael Jordan, at 15, was passed up for his high school basketball team.

Your true character is built not on whether you failed but on how and when you pick yourself back up again.

Embracing failure is the antidote for perfectionism, procrastination and playing small. You can't be perfect if you fail. Why chronically procrastinate when trying and possibly failing are something to look forward to? Giving it a go is great for building confidence and strengthening your self-esteem and thus playing a bigger game.

CREATIVITY

Best-selling author, Elizabeth Gilbert said in her *Magic Lessons* podcast that creativity is an irrational act. Essentially you are saying that you are going to take the single most valuable commodity you have—the irreplaceable currency of time—and devote it to making something that nobody wants, that nobody asked you to do, that nobody is waiting for, that might not work, and that you might not even like. Why in the world would you do that?

I have some answers to that deep question and they revolve around writing a novel in a month. In November 2016, I wrote my very first novel during National Novel Writing Month. This is a mouthful so it gets abbreviated to NaNoWriMo, which really is only slightly less of a mouthful. Each year, in November, thousands of writers around the world take up the challenge to write a 50,000-word (approximately 180 page) novel for NaNoWriMo. I can now count myself as a NaNoWriMo 'winner'. Winners succeed in getting 50,000 words written before the end of the month. Other participants have varying levels of success up to that lofty number. The point is to ignore your inner editor and plough on. Just get those words down. My silly little romance may never be seen by anyone else but it more or less contained elements that make it a complete—albeit draft—work of fiction.

So why create? Here are three reasons:

1. To try something that seems far too ambitious, ridiculous or pointless. Deciding to embark on a hard, challenging or passion-fueled task is often surprisingly fulfilling. It taps into that inner child in all of us.
2. To get into the 'flow state'. This is what humans want and need more of, and it is becoming increasingly rare these days with constant distractions only a tap of the finger away. In the throes of creativity, you can't help but be in flow, be really present. And it feels amazing.
3. To start something. It is perfectly okay to start something with absolutely no idea of how the process will go, how it should look or how on earth you are going to finish it. Trusting the creative process means letting yourself be pleasantly surprised by where the project takes you. I am a very organized person and thought I would have a perfect outline and screeds of character notes before I started NaNoWriMo. In fact, all I did was draw a giant mind map which I then proceeded to ignore and allowed my characters to take on a life of their own.

Like intuition, everyone is creative, but some people have lost their sense of it. You can relearn to be creative. Historical data shows that people are less depressed and have higher confidence the more they use their hands.

Try any or all of the following to strengthen your creativity muscle: cook, draw, paint, knit, sew, build, write songs, dance, decorate, make videos, brew beer, make soap, take up photography or of course, write a novel. Creativity is only limited by your imagination.

Creativity is not self-indulgent or trivial. It is one of the most important things we can do for ourselves and the planet. It reflects our awesomeness as creating stems from our uniqueness. Charles Pépin write in *Self-Confidence: A Philosophy* that "our thumbs glide over the surface of smart phones and we glide over the surface of things." We are not present in our bodies, not in touch with our senses anymore.

If going within is too woo-woo for you, then here is your answer: create something tangible. It is reassuring to make, master or finish something. The sourdough and banana bread baking trends during quarantine make complete sense.

Creativity allows us to meet ourselves once again.

And if those reasons above don't encourage you to create, then don't do it for yourself. Do it for others. You never know who your project will touch so don't give up on it. Just do it. Because I embraced my creativity and wrote a book, I was invited onto a virtual summit with a number of other women from different fields. A friend of mine, Georgie, inspired as a result of watching another interview, decided to start her own creative venture. As a thank you, she gave me a gorgeous crystal bracelet that she now makes as part of her business, Elegant Empowerment. Think about this for a second. I wrote a book and somewhere along the way, this helped someone to start a business.

Please don't deny your creativity for another second.

• • •

Dream Big

To dream big is to make every piece of your life the masterpiece it is meant to be because it doesn't matter how great your life is, there is another level—one of passion, gratitude, connection, joy and success.

Dreaming big is the very last awesomeness tool. It has purposely been left until last because you need to get a handle on the other tools before you truly adopt this one. Everything learned to date assists with dreaming big. You can't dream big if you are stuck in your immediate pleasure-seeking response and have no boundaries. Dreaming big means saying 'no' to something good now for the bigger prize later. And it won't happen unless you adore yourself and know you deserve a huge life simply because you are alive. Dreams will remain dreams unless you choose courage over comfort.

Desire has some funny connotations and seems controversial, but we all have desires and it is imperative we work out exactly what we want and go for it. Our need for certainty drops with every step out of our comfort zone and the world is richer as a result of our boldness.

Don't settle for mediocrity because you believe anything else is unavailable or inappropriate. Be rebellious. See what you can get away with. Not many people's opinions matter. So why not? When you go beyond expectations and what you think you are capable of, the world will open up. You will discover there is so much more you can do with your mind, body, skills and talents. You may even compel others to dream big too.

The best way to initiate dreaming big is to set yourself an audacious challenge. This appeals to an innate desire to excel, helps get you unstuck and taps into your best self. One morning, not long after I turned 39, I woke and up with a ridiculous idea: I could attempt to check off 40 bucket list items in the following year to mark my 40th birthday milestone.

My 'Top40 Bucket List' was born. Some items were cheap, local, and even dull. 'Grow sunflowers' was one item that would seem modest to others. Some I had to plan and budget for—traveling to another city to see 'The World of Wearable Arts' was one of the more expensive and time-consuming items. I definitely had to consider finances, family commitments and other constraints, but I had a list of 40 bucket list items I was intent on checking off. What a way to commemorate turning 40!

And as I write in *Bucket List Blueprint*, I did succeed in checking off every single one of the 40 bucket list items during that year. I ended on a literal high note when on the 30th of December, I jumped out of a plane in a tandem skydive. Doing my Top40 Bucket List was a mighty challenge, stressful and hard work at times, but I still feel extremely proud and satisfied that I crossed it all off.

Right now, with travel restrictions in place, this may seem like an impossible challenge. However, you can do a whole lot of stuff at home or in your local area. And nothing is stopping you from writing a bucket list for later. It doesn't even have to be a list. Name one challenge you would like to try before you 'kick the bucket' and start planning to make it happen.

Celebration

You have dreamed big, been creative, and, er, failed—now go and celebrate! Celebrating is another way of stepping out of your comfort zone. It can be tremendously fun as long as you don't allow your fear of what others may think of your 'bragging' to get in the way. It is also a way to pause and reflect and we all need a breather now and then. You need to celebrate YOU. If you don't, who else will? Repeat after me: "No one is going to give you a medal." Feel free to insert an expletive word before medal if you like. Remember, you are awesome! At the very least, celebrate your birthday.

A really fun way to celebrate is to spend a few minutes listing your accomplishments, challenges you have faced and your acts of kindness. All of them. Big and small. Over your whole life. That third place in long jump in the fifth grade. Managing to play that tricky piano solo in front of your grandmother. That first pay check. The university degree. Having a baby. Downsizing and traveling the world. Standing up for something you believe in. Telling someone you love them. Writing a note of thanks about your favorite waiter. Large successes such as climbing a mountain, writing a book or designing your dream home. Smaller, yet no less significant accomplishments such as getting out of bed and taking a shower when you were in the midst of a dark time. Write them all down. It will be a long list. Refer back to it often and give yourself a pat on the back or perform a little dance of joy every time you read it.

One thing you can celebrate is almost getting to the end of this book—only two short chapters to go.

Challenges

Try these challenges for the next 30 days and then decide which ones you want to continue with for the long term.

Challenge 1 – Fail: Ask yourself at the end of the day if you failed at anything (perhaps ask the family over dinner). If you have failed, then celebrate as it means you are trying.

Challenge 2 – Create: Decide to spend at least a few minutes each day creating something. This could be a different thing each day (e.g.: a meal or a picture) or something that is created over time like writing a novel, knitting a scarf or building a treehouse.

Challenge 3 – Dream big: Think of and start to plan one or more big life goals or challenges.

Bonus 'Anytime' Challenge – Write a list of all your accomplishments, big and small from over your entire life and celebrate how great you are.

11

THE PARADOX OF AWESOMENESS

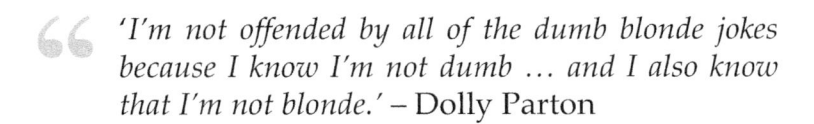

> 'I'm not offended by all of the dumb blonde jokes because I know I'm not dumb ... and I also know that I'm not blonde.' – Dolly Parton

Recap

Phew! Your head may be spinning. Let's do a quick review of the main points:

- Awesomeness is your birthright—you are awesome because you are alive
- You don't have to be or do anything to prove it—you are just awesome
- Unfortunately, we lose our sense of how awesome we really are due to our learned negative thought patterns and culturally conditioned beliefs
- Our prehistoric 'lizard' brain creates a real human need for safety, security, certainty, control, predictability and order
- As a result of this survival mechanism we learn

- two primary fears: that we are not enough and so won't be loved
- The bottom line of The Lizard + Certainty + Primary Fears equation is low self-love (which can also be called low self-worth or low self-esteem)
- This lack of self-love manifests in many ways, in particular: The Four Hazards
- The Four Hazards are Perfectionism, Procrastination, People Pleasing and Playing Small (which consists of low self-esteem, imposter syndrome, nagging self-doubt or lack of self-confidence)
- The Four Hazards (P's) can be minimized or eliminated by The Four Solutions (S's) which allow you to embrace your awesomeness once more
- The Four Solutions are Self-Love, Security and Control, Social Awesomeness and Step Out of Your Comfort Zone
- Each of The Four Solutions has three Tools of Awesomeness – 12 in total:

1. Awesomeness Pep Talk
2. Self-Love Affirmations
3. Practice Self-Care
4. Rituals and Habits
5. Empowering Language
6. Tap into Your Intuition
7. Say 'No'
8. Detach from Approval and Criticism
9. Better Communication
10. Fail
11. Create
12. Dream Big

All of this will also be listed in the Appendix for easy reference.

The Paradox of Awesomeness

What is being asked of you?

- Do everything you can to feel in control AND be able to live with uncertainty
- Love yourself just as you are AND be willing to grow into your potential
- Treat yourself with kindness AND challenge yourself to be better
- Be content with your life as it is AND strive to improve and grow
- Express your opinions clearly AND shut up and listen
- Stand your ground AND be adaptable
- Be sane in an insane world

Carl Jung calls paradoxes "one of our most valued spiritual possessions." I would call them a pain in the proverbial! They are by their very nature full of uncertainty so of course it's hard to accept them. Regardless, we must trust them and navigate them in order to live life to the full and embrace our awesomeness.

What is being asked is so simple, it's just that we are constantly looking around it instead of staring straight at the bat in the cage.

You have been asked to love yourself fully. You have been asked to show your real self to the world. You have been asked to step out of your comfort zone when you can.

These are all risky, vulnerable and uncertain requests. You are to go on a dark, painful journey… and for what? What can be promised in return? What is on the other side?

Deep down you know. You've felt empty for a long, long time. There is a void where you know something is missing, you have just forgotten what it is. The vague yearning feeling has been with you for as long as you can remember. You have been homesick for you.

Embracing your awesomeness means coming home.

It means coming back to your real self, your soul, your place in the universe.

Perhaps the biggest paradox of awesomeness is that what you have been longing for, what you have been homesick for has been within you all along. You wanted certainty and you wanted love and they have always been there for the taking.

Permission Slip

At the beginning of this book I gave you a permission slip. You can now tear it up. You don't need a permission slip from a book. You don't need it from me. You don't need it from anyone else. I will still be here cheering from the sidelines, but you've got this.

You ARE your own permission slip.

12

A WORLD OF AWESOMENESS

> *'And now that you don't have to be perfect, you can be good.'* – John Steinbeck

Quiz Time

Read the first set of questions, pause for a few seconds and then read the second set. There is no need to find out the actual answers. You won't be marked. Just read through the two quizzes and you will get the point.

First Quiz

1. Name the wealthiest person in the world
2. Name the last winner of the Miss America contest
3. Name the first person who won the Nobel Peace Prize
4. Name the director of the best picture at the Academy Awards last year
5. Name the person who got the most gold medals at the last Olympic games

Second Quiz

1. Name a teacher who helped you at school
2. Name a friend who assisted you through a tough time
3. Name three people who you enjoy spending quality time with
4. Name someone who taught you something that changed your life
5. Name one person who makes you feel loved, valued and appreciated

How did you do?

A World of Awesomeness

Imagine a world where we all embrace our innate awesomeness. What would it look like?

Sure, there would be the a few people in the first group. The ones who are the very best in the fields. The ones who are super-high achievers. The ones with the most credentials, the most money or the most awards. But in the end, we barely remember them.

What is more encouraging is the second group. This represents many unremarkable people, the ones the history books won't remember—you and me. The ones who decide to show up. The ones who love themselves enough to grow into their potential. The ones who don't let hazardous beliefs stop them from sharing their gifts. The ones who found joy, grace and beauty in the ordinary, every single day.

The ones who unreservedly embraced their awesomeness.

Become part of the second group.

Embrace your awesomeness.

Create a legacy.

Start today.

APPENDIX

Recap

- Awesomeness is your birthright—you are awesome because you are alive

- You don't have to be or do anything to prove it—you are just awesome

- Unfortunately, we lose our sense of how awesome we really are due to our learned negative thought patterns and culturally conditioned beliefs

- Our prehistoric 'lizard' brain creates a real human need for safety, security, certainty, control, predictability and order

- As a result of this survival mechanism we learn two primary fears: that we are not enough and so won't be loved

- The bottom line of The Lizard + Certainty +

Appendix

Primary Fears equation is low self-love (which can also be called low self-worth or low self-esteem)

- This lack of self-love manifests in many ways, in particular: The Four Hazards

- The Four Hazards are:

  - Perfectionism
  - Procrastination
  - People Pleasing
  - Playing Small (which consists of low self-esteem, imposter syndrome, nagging self-doubt or lack of self-confidence)

- The Four Hazards (P's) can be minimized or eliminated by The Four Solutions (S's) which allow you to embrace your awesomeness once more

- The Four Solutions are:

  - Self-Love
  - Security and Control
  - Social Awesomeness
  - Step Out of Your Comfort Zone

- Each of The Four Solutions has three Tools of Awesomeness – 12 in total:

1. Awesomeness Pep Talk
2. Self-Love Affirmations
3. Practice Self-Care
4. Rituals and Habits

5. Empowering Language
6. Tap into Your Intuition
7. Say 'No'
8. Detach from Approval and Criticism
9. Better Communication
10. Fail
11. Create
12. Dream Big

Monthly Challenges

Try these challenges for the next 30 days and then decide which ones you want to continue with for the long term.

- Awesomeness pep talk: read the awesomeness pep talk to yourself once per day.

- Self-love affirmations: say self-love affirmations to yourself in the mirror for one minute per day.

- Practice self-care: make a list of your favorite self-care activities and commit to doing at least one per day.

- Rituals and habits: decide to do one positive habit every day for the next month, e.g.: go for a 20-minute walk, have a bowl of raw vegetables before dinner, say thanks at every mealtime, make your bed or spend some time reading.

- Empowering language: change at least one disempowering word or phrase to an empowering one, e.g.: remove 'should' from your vocabulary. Simply don't say those negative words. The Lizard might still think them, but don't say them out loud. I doubt anyone will notice as they are too busy rushing around being stressed. But you will feel a difference.

- Tap into your intuition: add in a daily stillness habit: pause, breathe deeply, walk in nature, meditate or sit in silence and notice your five physical senses in order to make space for you to tap into your intuition.

- Say 'no': say a polite 'no' every day—to your partner, kids, friends, work colleagues, charities, committees, sales people and anyone else who comes along. Remember 'no' is a complete sentence.

- Detach from approval and criticism: practice ignoring opinions of those who do not matter (95% of the world) and saying a simple 'thanks' to any other feedback you receive in the next month.

- Better communication: be vigilant at reworking as much of your communication as possible into warm, direct and assertive sentences, using I statements, consequences and asking for exactly what you want.

- Fail: Ask yourself at the end of the day if you failed at anything (perhaps ask the family over dinner). If you have failed, then celebrate as it means you are trying.

- Create: Decide to spend at least a few minutes each day creating something. This could be a different thing each day (e.g.: a meal or a picture)

Appendix

or something that is created over time like writing a novel, knitting a scarf or building a treehouse.

- Dream big: Think of and start to plan one or more big life goals or challenges.

Bonus 'Anytime' Challenges

- Decide on your go-to extravagant compliment. Write it down and say it out loud three times whenever you are being critical of yourself.

- Adopt some practical habits you want to set up and continue with on, say, a monthly basis, e.g.: reviewing your expenses, installing a regular date night or volunteering.

- Use the phrase 'tell me more' when it is the very last thing you want to do during a tough conversation or argument.

- Write a list of all your accomplishments, big and small from over your entire life and celebrate how great you are.

If you get nothing else out of this book, then instead of asking, 'Is this true?', ask 'Is this helpful?'

READER GIFT: THE HAPPY20

Part of embracing your awesomeness is remembering to squeeze the best out every single day. To remind you of this, I created:

THE HAPPY20
20 Free Ways to Boost Happiness in 20 Seconds or Less

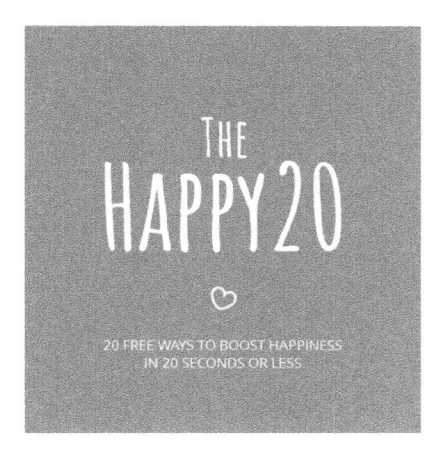

A PDF gift for you with quick ideas to improve your mood and add a little sparkle to your day.

Head to **JulieSchooler.com/gift** to grab your copy today.

AWESOMENESS ALERT!
When you enter your details for The Happy20 gift you will now get a second bonus gift.
This is an Awesomeness Pep Talk - a one-page PDF designed to be printed out so you can read it often.

Don't wait. Grab BOTH gifts today!
JulieSchooler.com/gift

ABOUT THE AUTHOR

Julie had aspirations of being a writer since she was very young but somehow got sidetracked into the corporate world. After the birth of her first child, she rediscovered her creative side. You can find her at JulieSchooler.com.

Her *Easy Peasy* books provide simple and straightforward information on parenting topics. The *Nourish Your Soul* series shares delicious wisdom to feel calmer, happier and more fulfilled.

Busy people can avoid wasting time searching for often confusing and conflicting advice and instead spend time with the beautiful tiny humans in their lives and do what makes their hearts sing.

Julie lives with her family in a small, magnificent country at the bottom of the world where you may find her trying to bake the perfect chocolate brownie.

BOOKS BY JULIE SCHOOLER

Easy Peasy Books
Easy Peasy Potty Training
Easy Peasy Healthy Eating

Nourish Your Soul Books
Rediscover Your Sparkle
Crappy to Happy
Embrace Your Awesomeness
Bucket List Blueprint
Super Sexy Goal Setting
Find Your Purpose in 15 Minutes
Clutter-Free Forever

Children's Picture Books
Maxy-Moo Flies to the Moon

Collections
Change Your Life 3-in-1 Collection
Rebelliously Happy 3-in-1 Collection

JulieSchooler.com/books

ACKNOWLEDGMENTS

I could not have written this book without the consistent and unwavering support of a small bunch of people I have never met in real life (hopefully one day, Cat!): the #Gr8Blogs Mastermind Group. Thank you for your encouragement and love from all four corners of the world.

To Peter from Toastmasters. Thanks for telling me I had a voice all those years ago. Without your informal mentoring, I may not have started writing books, let alone be publishing my tenth! You are a primary example of someone who has embraced his awesomeness.

To Andrew and our two beautiful tiny humans, Dylan and Eloise. I live in a perpetual state of astonishment about how fortunate my life is. Thank you for making me laugh every single day.

PLEASE LEAVE A REVIEW

Embrace Your Awesomeness

Feel in Control and Be Your Best Self in this Banana-Pants Crazy World

THANK YOU FOR READING THIS BOOK

I devoted many months to researching and writing this book. I then spent more time having it professionally edited, working with a designer to create an awesome cover and launching it into the world.

Time, money and heart has gone into this book and I very much hope you enjoyed reading it as much as I loved creating it.

It would mean the world to me if you could spend a few minutes writing a review on Goodreads or the online store where you purchased this book.

Please Leave a Review

A review can be as short or long as you like and should be helpful and honest to assist other potential buyers of the book.

Reviews provide social proof that people like and recommend the book. More book reviews mean more book sales which means I can write more books.

Your book review helps me, as an independent author, more than you could ever know. I read every single review and when I get five-star review it absolutely makes my day.

Thanks, Julie.

REFERENCES

Resources

This book is a result of extensive research using various websites, articles, blog posts, podcasts and TEDx talks, too numerous to list here.

Books

59 Seconds – Change Your Life in Under a Minute – Richard Wiseman (USA, 2011)

Atomic Habits – An Easy and Proven Way to Build Good Habits and Break Bad Ones – James Clear (US, 2018)

Authentic Happiness – Using the New Positive Psychology to Realize Your Potential for Lasting Fulfillment – Martin Seligman, Ph.D. (US, 2002)

Braving the Wilderness – The Quest for True Belonging and the Courage to Stand Alone – Brené Brown, Ph.D. (US, 2017)

References

Daring Greatly – How the Courage to Be Vulnerable Transforms the Way We Live, Love, Parent and Lead – Brené Brown, Ph.D. (US, 2012)

Do Less – A Revolutionary Approach to Time and Energy Management for Busy Moms – Kate Northrup (US, 2019)

Embracing Uncertainty – Achieving Peace of Mind as We Face the Unknown – Susan Jeffers, Ph.D. (US, 2003)

Essentialism – The Disciplined Pursuit of Less – Greg McKeown (US, 2014)

Feel the Fear and Do It Anyway – How to Turn Your Fear and Indecision into Confidence and Action – Susan Jeffers (UK, 1987)

Finding Your Own North Star – How to Claim the Life You Were Meant to Live – Martha Beck (US, 2001)

Finding Your Way in a Wild New World – Reclaim Your True Nature to Create the Life You Want – Martha Beck (US, 2012)

Girl, Stop Apologizing – A Shame-Free Plan for Embracing and Achieving Your Goals – Rachel Hollis (US, 2019)

Girl, Wash Your Face – Stop Believing the Lies About Who You Are So You Can Become Who You Were Meant to Be – Rachel Hollis (US, 2018)

Happy for No Reason – 7 Steps to Being Happy from the Inside Out – Marci Shimoff (USA, 2008)

References

How to Be an Imperfectionist – The New Way to Self-Acceptance, Fearless Living and Freedom from Perfectionism – Stephen Guise (US, 2015)

How to Win Friends and Influence People – Dale Carnegie (USA, 1953 /2006)

Love Yourself Like Your Life Depends On It – Kamal Ravikant (US, 2020)

Man's Search for Meaning – Victor E. Frankl (US, 1959 / 2006)

Minimalism – Live a Meaningful Life – Joshua Fields Millburn and Ryan Nicodemus (US, 2016)

On Being Human – A Memoir of Waking Up, Living Real and Listening Hard – Jennifer Pastiloff (US, 2019)

Playing Big – Find Your Voice, Your Vision and Make Things Happen – Tara Mohr (US, 2014)

Radical Acceptance – Awakening the Love that Heals Fear and Shame Within Us – Tara Brach (US, 2003)

Rising Strong – The Reckoning. The Rumble. The Revolution. – Brené Brown, Ph.D. (US, 2015)

Rushing Woman's Syndrome – The Impact of a Never-Ending To-Do List on your Health – Dr. Libby Weaver (NZ, 2011)

Self-Confidence – A Philosophy – Charles Pépin (UK, 2020)

Steering by Starlight – The Science and Magic of Finding Your Destiny – Martha Beck (US, 2008)

Stop Trying So F*cking Hard – Live Authentically, Design a Life You Love, and Be Happy (Finally)! – Honorée Corder (US, 2018)

The Choice – Embrace the Possible – Dr. Edith Eva Eger (US, 2017)

The Confidence Code – The Science and Art of Self-Assurance – What Women Should Know – Katty Kay and Claire Shipman (US, 2014)

The Dance of Anger – A Woman's Guide to Changing the Patterns of Intimate Relationships – Harriet Lerner, Ph.D. (US, 1985 / 2016)

The Dance of Intimacy – A Woman's Guide to Courageous Acts of Change in Key Relationships – Harriet Lerner, Ph.D. (US, 1990 / 1999)

The Gifts of Imperfection – Let Go of Who You Think You're Supposed to Be and Embrace Who You Are – Brené Brown, Ph.D. (US, 2010)

The Happiness Project – Gretchen Rubin (USA, 2009)

The ONE Thing – The Surprisingly Simple Truth Behind Extraordinary Results – Gary Keller with Jay Papasan (US, 2013)

The Power is Within You – Louise Hay (US, 1991 / 2006 / 2017)

The Secret – Rhonda Byrne (US, 2006)

The Seven Habits of Highly Effective People – Restoring the Character Ethic – Steven R Covey (US, 1990)

*The Subtle Art of Not Giving a F*ck* – *A Counterintuitive Approach to Living a Good Life* – Mark Manson (US, 2016)

The Top Five Regrets of the Dying – *A Life Transformed by the Dearly Departed* – Bronnie Ware (US, 2011)

The Winner's Bible – *Rewire Your Brain for Permanent Change* – Dr. Kerry Spackman (USA, 2009)

Thrive – *The Third Metric to Redefining Success and Creating a Life of Wellbeing, Wisdom and Wonder* – Arianna Huffington (US, 2014)

Tools of Titans: The Tactics, Routines, and Habits of Billionaires, Icons, and World-Class Performers – Tim Ferriss (US, 2016)

You are a Badass – *How to Stop Doubting Your Greatness and Start Living an Awesome Life* – Jen Sincero (US, 2013)

Printed in Great Britain
by Amazon